SEEING OTHERS SUCCESSFUL

THE JOY OF ELEVATING PEOPLE

BY JOSEPH A. ROGOWSKI

Publisher's Name: Joseph A. Rogowski

ISBN: 978-1-962142-80-9

Bible reference abbreviations are as follows: NIV- New International Version, Holman Publishers 1986; NKJV-OB New King James Version Open Bible, Nelson Publishers1985; NAB-New American Bible, Catholic Book Publishing 1970; KJV-King James Version; KJV-pt - KJV paraphrased translation.

Table of Contents

ACKNOWLEDGMENTS

Although this manual may be considered small by many standards, it was a significant project requiring considerable energy and dedication. It is born out of years of interaction with teachers, students, seminar attendees, and workers in the ministry of community development.

Sifting through voluminous notes and recollections to shape this into a manageable text was only possible with the loving encouragement, devotion, and cheer of my wife, Ursula.

Special recognition goes to the leaders of the many Youth with a Mission training centers on several continents, as well as Pastor Paul Swarr. They allowed me to share the vision and principles of community development ministry in their training sessions and at various pastor's conferences, Bible schools, and university settings.

Sincere appreciation goes to Dr. John Munday of Chesapeake, Virginia for his friendship and invaluable guidance and editing of the manuscript with his typical patience, candor, and expertise. Thanks also go to Pastor Jim Booth of Glen Allen, Virginia, for his knowledgeable critique. Any residual flaws or errors in the text are completely and totally incumbent on myself.

Above all, I praise the Lord for guiding me through to the successful completion of this manual.

Joe Rogowski

Butterfly artwork by Daniel J. Mey

INTRODUCTION

This manual should prove useful to all who work with groups of people, communities, or even nations, as the principles espoused here have universal application. It is not intended to be a scholarly work as much as it is a beginner's look at first principles in working with the disadvantaged. We present a framework for those interested to be more effective in their vocations with varied groups whatever they may be.

The use of religious parallels and illustrations is fundamental here since the principles presented are grounded in biblical concepts and truth. However, they do not simply apply to ministry workers. This book can serve as a valuable resource for organization leaders, educators, and business professionals. Others, of course, may adapt these ideas to their own situations and circumstances.

For the first eight years of my mission work, I had a gnawing sense that my ministry was never fully successful due to some inexplicable lack. How could I focus on winning souls in places where an entire nation might be burdened with poverty and need? The concept of "community development" in ministering to the poor brought renewed vision and expectation to my mission work.

The history of missions has been generally to give things to and do things for the poor. After all, isn't that what Jesus enjoins us to do? Yet, after many years of this approach, many poor communities have remained just as poor as when the missionaries first arrived.

We have misunderstood some basic principles in combating poverty and how people grow and develop to self-sufficiency. The ministries of doling out goods and services and doing things for them, in many ways, have been detrimental to the very people we have been trying to help.

In these pages, our aim is to promote the perspective that under suitable conditions real progress can come from stimulating and facilitating poor communities to help themselves. Development is not an event or an episode but a process. The process is much slower and painstaking but long-term sustainable results will prove the effectiveness of the approach.

To support this claim, a case will be made on a scriptural basis for "development" as a legitimate ministry option.

A corollary case will be made to address the hesitation or even reluctance to help the poor in concern that, historically, social justice programs have slowed the task of preaching the gospel and saving the lost.

Some of the ideas expressed here are not original. Due to the accumulation of notes over many years used in composing this manuscript, it remains a challenge to identify which ideas are original to the author and which were drawn from outside sources—and specifically from whom. These ideas have been acquired through decades of sitting in lectures, forums, hearing sermons, other readings on the subject, personal reflection, and even from simple conversations with like-minded people attempting in our efforts to define workable strategies for ministering to the poor.

Whenever possible, credits are happily bestowed on those individuals from whom ideas expressed here are realized. Dr. Merrill Ewert's course on the *Principles of Community Development* reinforced our confidence that community development, when properly understood leads to sustainable and long-range results. Peter Batchelor's book *People in Rural Development* and Ralph Bunch's *Two Ears of Corn*, were also particularly helpful.

When not possible to identify sources due to a lack of information, knowledge, or recollection, we make the full assumption that the ideas actually did originate with the author or do appear at least in some enlarged or revised form from the original.

At the outset, we acknowledge the sources that were clearly influential in the formulation of this manuscript, even if we cannot fully identify or cite their specific contributions.

Seminal thoughts on LUKE 2:52 - by Bob Moffitt
The Development Ethic - by Darrow Miller
The Gift That Releases - by Dr. John Steward
Principles of Community Development - by Dr. D. Merrill Ewert
Two Ears of Corn - by Roland Bunch
People in Rural Development - by Peter Batchelor
Church Planting Through Obedience Oriented Teaching - by George Patterson
Readings from Solomon Islands Development Trust (SIDT) - by Henry T. Samani

In the personal anecdotes throughout the book, names of most individuals have been changed to protect their privacy. Our inability to locate some for their expressed permission to use their names made it necessary to change their names here, but not all.

DEDICATION

This manual is dedicated to the Ghanaian brethren who believed in me over a period of nearly two decades by embracing and propagating the principles of community development as foundational outreach ministry for their communities and their nation: Nick and Grace Oddoye, Paul and Gladys Agyemang, Joseph Mensah, Eric Wussah, Godfred Kwakye, Joseph Nii and Betty Ankrah.

To Pastor Sampson and Janet Dorkunor of Living Bread Mission, Ashaiman, Ghana and Edwin and Esther Gbor, directors of The Great Commission Fundamental Baptist Mission, Ganta, Liberia for their friendship and ardent service to the Lord.

To John Bills and Dean Sherman of the USA, and to Dr. Bruce Thompson of New Zealand, each for their unique act of kindness at a moment in time.

PREFACE

JOB 29:1-25

This passage of Scripture is remarkable for its placement. It is one of those rich deposits found in a seemingly unexpected place in Scripture.

Job laments the good old days when he held a prominent place in his community. His stature among his neighbors was such that when young people were in his presence, because of his reputation and influence, they withdrew into the background. The fact that the aged and elders stood at his arrival was especially significant in a culture that revered and respected age, yet they rose to their feet for him.

In verse 9, the chief men became speechless at his arrival covering their mouths as if struck dumb. Aristocrats were silenced in his presence unable to swallow from dryness of mouth. In verses 11 and throughout 21-25, we're told that the only things worth their attention or consideration were Job's counsel and wisdom and receiving his smile of reassurance. The reasons why all these things were true of Job in his community should deeply move us.

All these things were true of Job because he delivered the poor who cried for help and the orphan who had no caring support. He brought comfort to the dying and made the hearts of widows sing. Integrity and fairness were as natural to Job as putting on garments. He was eyes to the blind, feet to the lame, and a tower to the poor and when the occasion arose, in confrontations with injustice, he even took up their cause. Job was the ultimate Old Testament expression of salt and light to his community and became a dominating influence in his society.

MATT 5:16 - *"Let your light so shine before men that they may see your good works and glorify your Father in heaven."* **NKJV-OB**

While my wife and I were leading a discipleship training school in Powhatan, Virginia, Gayle Erwin[1] was one of our invited speakers. In the middle of one of his humorous presentations, he stopped abruptly, changed the direction of his speaking, and said very seriously, if we ever want to feel uncomfortable or feel disconcerted, when we read the Scriptures pay close attention to how frequently and with what intensity God mentions "the poor." Pay close attention to how frequently God[1] mentions things like the widow, the orphan, the naked, the homeless, the hungry, the needy, the oppressed.

---

[1]Gayle D. Erwin – Director of Servant Quarters, author of The Jesus Style. http://www.servant.org/

Gayle's remarks were so disjointed from his earlier funny comments that he seemed peculiarly out of place. But he was serious. Quickly, he was back to his old humorous form, picking up on his previous topic and lecturing on. I was left behind in my thoughts, reflecting on his remarks about God and the poor. I was being changed. I was being impacted because I took up his suggestion.

From that point on, whenever I read Scripture, I began to pay closer attention to how often and intensely God mentions "the poor." Mentions are everywhere - in Genesis, Leviticus, Psalms, Proverbs, the Prophets, indeed, throughout the whole of the Old Testament, dispelling the notion that "loving our neighbor" was some New Testament concept that had arrived with Jesus.

I was moved by recollections of my own insensitivity and neglect of something that was so obviously a matter on God's heart. More than that, I began to catch the vision of how the Great Love Commandment was actually a vehicle for fulfilling the Great Commission.

Many times I have been filled with feelings of remorse and self-condemnation for not having the quick, automatic, compassionate response to people's needs, as others do, but rather go through a lumbering, analytical approach before responding. Yet, having this slow type safety-valve response can give us time to reflect on the best response for those in need. Giving-to or doing-for someone automatically might not be the best response for them. Some stimulation to a self-help approach might be a better idea. It's much like raising our children. In misguided compassion, we can do things for them and give things to them in such a way as to hinder their development in becoming responsible and mature persons.

We aim to present the case that there is a definitive pattern for human development and for human activity as developers. In mission circles, the term *community development* has come to signify the improvement toward self-reliance or self-sufficiency - the militating forces countering dependency. Dependency, time and again, has proven to be damaging to human creative initiative and to the human spirit overall.

Giving to and doing for people from an insensible motive that does not regard the detrimental effect it might have on their development can increase the number of poor instead of alleviating their condition. In the spirit of community, if we can lead them to a Quality-of-Life just a notch higher than where they presently are by bringing some improvement, without creating a dependency, we would be on the road to *Development* and self-reliance.

Clearly, this places a serious demand on community development practitioners who will be tested to fulfill the various roles required in facilitating the *process* of development. The process involves people taking control of their lives and futures, embarking on an upward spiral of improvement through collective action to break the cycle of poverty.

CHAPTER ONE: REPRESENTING THE KINGDOM RIGHTLY

There is controversy within Christianity over which command is more important, the command to love God or the command to love our neighbor. Some maintain that we cannot be saved unless we love God, while others claim that loving our neighbor is the actual proof we love God and so it cannot be minimized. If this controversy lingers in our own hearts, it will affect how we minister to others.

In Jesus' own words, in LUKE 4:16-19, His entire ministry was intended to impact the poor. His entire "anointing" was directed toward the poor.

Entire nations are poor and most of those nations are what would be considered in Christian circles "lost," that is, without a notable Christian presence. Preaching and witnessing will always have their place but if we are going to reach nations for Jesus, with needs so great; our Christianity has got to be relevant to their situation.

PSM 2:8 - *"Ask of me and I will give you the nations for your inheritance."*
NKJV-OB

In our endeavor to encourage confidence in the principles discussed in this book we will hold fast to MATT 5:16 as our standard motto for soul winning with its resultant promise that as we exhibit good works, men will come to the Lord and give glory to Him.

"Let your light so shine before men that they may see your good works and glorify your Father in heaven." **NKJV-OB**

****

PSM 89:14 - "*Righteousness and justice are the foundation of your throne..*"
NKJV-OB

There are two elements to God's throne. One without the other misrepresents the Kingdom of God and can cause an imbalance to our ministry approach. We can so emphasize righteousness issues that we neglect justice or so emphasize justice and social issues that we overlook the righteous demands of the Gospel.

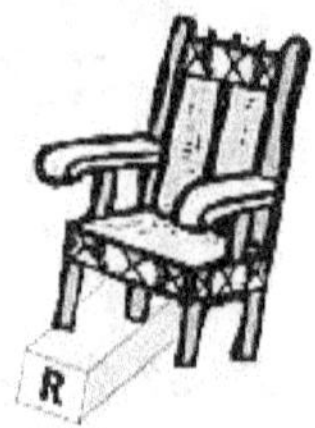

Generally, the two most frequently mentioned sins in the Bible are ***idolatry*** and ***injustice***. Idolatry violates the command to love God, while injustice violates the command to love our neighbor. The Bible teaches that loving God is righteousness and loving our neighbor is justice - injustice being those things we do to one another, such as lying, stealing, cheating, infidelity, violence, murder.

If we decide that spiritual matters are more important in God's plan, we may focus on evangelism, church planting, and discipleship, potentially neglecting the practical needs of others. We can display damaging attitudes in our disposition to others through *indifference and insensitivity* to their deprivation. In our rush and earnestness to "lead someone to the Lord" we can appear callous in our spirituality with a seeming lack of compassion for people's physical needs.

On the other hand, if we believe that "loving our neighbor" is the more important thing, we may focus on justice and mercy ministries and risk neglecting the spiritual needs of people. The prospect of facing a hostile response or opposition when sharing a Gospel message can be uncomfortable.

Often the poor are regarded as too vulnerable or disadvantaged to be approached with something as challenging and serious as a Gospel message. Workers may believe that in helping the poor they would be imposing on them or exploiting them by sharing the Gospel somewhat akin to promoting a hidden agenda. Some denominations, as a matter of policy, do not even allow the ministries of "helping the poor" and "evangelism" to function together, regarding the two as separate ministries not to be ministered conjunctively.

While on a lunch break at the Phanat Nikom refugee camps in Thailand in the early eighties, a young female UN worker approached me directly to my face and accused me with some vehemence of being an "opportunist." We Christians take these opportunities to pounce on the refugees in their weakness and misery and try to convert them to our religion was her allegation.

Startled into a deep embarrassing pause, I finally responded by suggesting that she was absolutely right – that I was an opportunist. In fact, as Christians we wanted to be there first to bring a message of hope, comfort, and healing to these people in their misery before they sought other means of comfort to lessen their pain like drugs, alcohol, sex or any other kind of destructive immoral and social behavior.

Sadly, I did not have the presence of mind to remind her that we Christians were there also to clean the latrines of the refugees, distribute clothing, food rations, potable water and blankets, while providing them with mail services in that remote area, and teaching them rudimentary technical skills.

Our sixteen-year-old daughter Sylvia worked in clothing distribution, our fourteen-year-old son Alex in water distribution and my wife Ursula ran the postal service – all of us as unpaid missionary volunteers while that young lady was serving there in some UN capacity on a somewhat comfortable income.

One's sense of balance can be skewed by an attitude that "idealizes" the poor. We speculate that "the poor" are somehow sanctified or ennobled because of their "humble" circumstances. Experience has shown that the poor are themselves in need of the gospel to repent of their wrongdoings and reform their lives just as much as anyone else. One would only need to have observed how some, not all, of the refugees in the Thailand transit camps during the early *1980s* treated each other. In their meager, wretched circumstances, one would have thought that the refugees would have been more closely knit together in community. Yet, in many situations, they would steal each other's blankets, clothing, mail, or even food to gain some type of advantage.

As much as Jesus had compassion on the poor, it was because they were powerless, in such want, or victims of some injustice, and not because they were inherently righteous. Jesus nonetheless, fully in accord with His character, despite their wrongdoing, calls us to be obedient to Him and to help them in their plight. While there may be controversy in Christendom over which Commandment is more important, to love God or to love our neighbor, there was never any controversy in the heart of Jesus. He would minister to the need as the need arose, whether it required a spiritual response or a physical one. His was a totally integrated ministry. A closer look at the Great Commission may help eliminate some of the controversy over which is really the more important command - to love God or to love our neighbor.

WHAT REALLY IS THE GREAT COMMISSION ANYWAY?

MATT 28:19-20 - *"Therefore go and make disciples of all nations, baptizing them in the name of the Father and of the Son and of the Holy Spirit and teaching them to obey everything I have commanded you. And surely I am with you always, to the very end of the age"* ***NIV***

There are two basic imperatives here: go and make disciples (preaching) and teaching them to obey. Readers often regard the first element to go and make disciples (or preach the Gospel) as being the all-inclusive, absolute injunction and stop there. We become so intent on the forepart of this command that we overlook the remainder of what Jesus said when He continued with the additional command "and teach them to obey." TEACH THEM TO OBEY WHAT? Teach them to obey what He has commanded! What are the commands of Jesus?

George Patterson, in his excellent teaching on church planting methods called TEEE[2] suggested that all the teachings, instructions, and admonitions of Jesus can be simplified and summarized into ***seven basic commands***. The list can be a quick check on our own obedience to the commands of Jesus as our testimony to being His followers. This simplified list can be used to teach those, who in situations where they may not be able to read or write, to remember it easily for teaching others and spreading the message. Remembering a short list like this would facilitate their learning and obedience and aid their capability in retelling the commands of Jesus, especially where illiteracy is a problem.

THE SEVEN BASIC COMMANDS OF JESUS:

1) Repent/believe
2) Be baptized
3) Pray
4) Give
5) Lord's Supper
6) Love - God, neighbor, enemies
7) Witness - "Go"

1) REPENT/BELIEVE - This command of Jesus has two elements that function together. Among the first words from Jesus as He entered public ministry were "Repent" and "Believe." They are the entry point into the family of believers.

---

2 George Patterson – Church Planting Through Obedience Oriented Teaching (Pasadena CA: William Carey Library,1981) p. 1

We' re told by Jesus to repent of our former lives and believe that He is who He said He is - the Savior of the world. He has come not to condemn us but to save us from our wrongdoing. Repentance is the admission that we are sinners who have made selfish, ungodly choices. We resolve to take a stand against our sinful behavior that will manifest itself in a change toward godly behavior. Without serious repentance as a lifestyle, obedience to the other commands of Jesus will lack determination, commitment and power.

Believing in Jesus is critical, as our forgiveness is appropriated through our faith in Him because of the salvation that was instituted through His death on the cross. If we believe, His substitution for us in accepting the punishment for our wrongdoing and his resurrected life remove the indictments against us.

2) BE BAPTIZED - Jesus commanded us to be baptized. This is the entry point into the church. It is the outward testimony of our faith in Jesus. It has no saving power of its own but becomes the outward and public testimony of our repentance and belief that Jesus is the Lord of our lives and of our commitment to conduct our lives in obedience to Him.

In cultures where Christianity has a major presence, baptism can be somewhat taken for granted and be treated as a routine observance. But in cultures intolerant of Christianity, it may be regarded as a prohibited practice. Submission to the rite of baptism is the open testimony of intention to follow Jesus in obedient faith. It can provoke vehement opposition, anger, jealousy, and threats in the environment of the religious culture that the convert is forsaking.

Christians need a greater revelation of the power of this important ritual and the true meaning that it holds for their testimony as followers of Jesus.

3) PRAY - Jesus commanded us to pray. He even told us how. Prayer is our communication link to God and is a reflection of our dependence on Him. The more we pray the greater our dependence, while the less we pray the greater our independence which is not a healthy state for a Christian. A prayer -less life smacks too much of presumption and pride with which the Lord cannot be pleased.

In the prayer, commonly called the Lord's Prayer, are broadly included generic elements of endearment, homage, acknowledgment of His sovereignty, worship, supplication, and repentance.

4) GIVE - Jesus commanded us to give. The poor are not exempt from giving according to Kingdom of God principles. Giving is a pathway to receiving. Jesus used a poor widow as an illustration of faith and sacrifice in giving, remarking that she gave "*out of her poverty.*" Her poverty was no excuse to refrain from giving.

MARK 12:44 - *"They all gave out of their wealth; but she, out of her poverty, put in everything - all she had to live on."* **NIV**

The poor can always find something to give whether it's a loaf of bread, veggies, or a bundle of eggs. Difficult as it may seem, the poor are to be instructed to give as a Kingdom principle.

5) LORD'S SUPPER - LUKE 22:19 - "*...do this in remembrance of me.*" **NIV**

Jesus commanded us to celebrate the remembrance of His death and what it means to our relationship with Him. We reflect on the *past* as to what He has done for us in removing the indictments against us; the *present,* as to where we now stand with Him in power at the right hand of the Father. Finally, we call to mind the *future* aspects of His return and the prospect of living with Him in eternity forever.

6) LOVE - There is no escaping this one. We must love God. Some people struggle with the notion that they love God because they sense no special surge of emotion in their feelings. They can be filled with doubts and fears that they are failing in this area. But there is great hope, since loving God is not a sensation or an emotion but a choice of heart, will, and mind as defined by obedience. Obedience to His commands is the indicator of loving God.

JOHN 14:21 - *"He who has My commandments and keeps them, it is he who loves Me."* **NKJV-OB**

The indisputable sign and testimony of our love for God is not in our emotional highs but in our obedience. An obedient faith to His commands is what the Lord cherishes.

In a major way, too, we are commanded to love our neighbor.

GAL 5:13-14 - "You, my brothers, were called to be free. But do not use your freedom to indulge the sinful nature rather, serve one another in love. The entire law is summed up in a single command: 'Love your neighbor as yourself.'" ***NIV***

According to Paul, the entirety of the law is summed up in a single command, *"Love your neighbor as yourself."* It is this entreaty that is commanded in detail throughout Scripture yet, many of us treat it as if were some kind of option.

The concept of "loving our neighbor" has too often been limited by our narrow, faulty vision. Our neighbor, as described in the Good Samaritan story, is not just the person next door, but anyone in need along with the broadened view of our neighborhood, community, city, state, country, and planet as our "collective neighbor."

****

Enhancing the welfare of our communities is a noble aspiration for Christians in obedience to the command to love our neighbor. If Christians are the guardians of truth as embodied in Jesus, then they ought to be in the forefront of the marketplace of ideas affecting community activity, policy, legislation, laws, direction, tradition, and our culture and custom safeguards. Forsaking societal, civic, and political debate to the designs, whims and arbitrary decisions of those harboring self-serving inclinations can lead to the disintegration of our culture and communities. Worse, we become complicit in the erosion of true and lasting values in our communities by our passivity and apathy. That would be a sad commentary on our performance as Christians in loving our neighbor.

I once had a man of the cloth suggest to me that, as a minister, political discourse was not "within his obligation."

If Jesus is Lord of all, He is certainly meant to be Lord of our social and political order. Service to the nation is not outside the "obligation" of the church as 2 CHR 7:13-14 reveals to us. These verses are addressed to believers. Repentance by God's people leads to healing of the land. These verses put the onus of rebuilding the nation on the believing church. They also provide support for the enlarged interpretation of "loving our neighbor," as having the equivalency of loving the nation as our collective neighbor.

In the following passage, we see another summary statement wherein Paul declares that the totality of the demands of the law is equal to the one command to love our neighbor as ourselves.

> *ROM 13:8-9 - "Let no debt remain outstanding, except the continuing debt to love one another, for he who loves his fellowman has fulfilled the law. The commandments, 'Do not commit adultery,' 'Do not murder,' 'Do not steal,' 'Do not covet,' and whatever other commandment there may be, are summed up in this one rule: 'Love your neighbor as yourself.'"* **NIV**

Paul includes a surprising expansion on his point by using the open-ended expression *"and whatever other commandment there may be."* He asserts that all the commandments we have now, any that we may not know about yet or any command that may still come down in the future is and will be summarized in the one command to *"love your neighbor as yourself."*

Most people would probably suggest that an eye for an eye and tooth for a tooth was the prevailing worldview of the Old Testament. The supposed, overturning principle to it came with Jesus when He made the radical statement that we were to love our neighbor as ourselves. Jesus was not bringing a revolutionary new concept but was reminding us that the command has always been on God's heart with this surprising gem in the Old Testament:

LEV 19:18 - *"Do not seek revenge or bear a grudge against one of your people but love your neighbor as yourself...."* **NIV**

Some people wonder how it's possible to love others when they have difficulty loving themselves. They have a depreciable or inadequate sense of being lovable. Jesus never commanded us to love ourselves. Perhaps He took it for granted because of our intrinsic worth. We could be assured of being lovable with a greater understanding of our value, dignity, and worth that come to us in being made in the image of God. The testimony of the infinite price that was paid to gain redemption for us, made possible by the death of Jesus on the cross, is supreme evidence of our worth. This greater understanding of the value and worth of humanity ought to elevate our thinking toward our aging, disabled, and unborn.

JAMES 2:8 - *"If you really keep the royal law found in Scripture, 'Love your neighbor as yourself,' you will be doing right."* **NIV**

James uses a rare descriptive term by calling the law "royal." A law is only deemed royal when it comes directly from the king, himself. In this case, the king is none other than the King of kings, King Jesus, who maintains His sovereign prerogative over the command that we are to love our neighbor as ourselves.

We're reminded also through the golden rule:

MATT 7:12 - "*So in everything, do to others what you would have them do to you, for this sums up the Law and the Prophets."* **NIV**

Finally, the commands to love don't stop with loving God and loving neighbor. We are also commanded to love our enemies - difficult, but nonetheless imperative. Opposition and hostility to Christianity is everywhere and appears to be accelerating.

Loving our enemies can be a formidable weapon that we have as Christians against opposition. The primary key to getting along with our enemies is to live a life that is pleasing to God.

PROV 16:7 - *"When a man's ways please the Lord, He makes even his enemies be at peace with him."* **NKJV-OB**

The combination of living a life pleasing to God and loving our tormentors, difficult though it may be, is a potent force in our arsenal. Implied in this command is the suggestion that we are to be peacemakers in our relationships.

7) WITNESS - All four Gospels have some form of command to go and share our faith. Despite the Scriptural evidence that supports the relationship between the two commandments there is a wide segment of Christianity that still treats the Great Commandment, to love our neighbor, as if it were some kind of option. We can fail to understand the full power inherent in loving our neighbor and the impact it can have in being His witnesses. Demonstrating the Gospel through loving our neighbor with practical helps can be a greater testimony than the pure act of proclamation.

JOHN 5:36 - *"But I have a greater witness than John's; for the works which the Father has given Me to finish, the very works that I do bear witness of Me, that the Father has sent Me."* **NKJV-OB**

Jesus does not minimize the importance of John's preaching. Preaching has its vital place and importance. Non-believers need to hear, believe, and come to faith. Yet, while Jesus is affirming of John, there is still a greater testimony than John's preaching and it is the **"*works that I do.*"** His works were the greater witness. We have relegated demonstrating the Gospel to some type of secondary, lesser evangelism even though it is under-girded by the promise that it will actually win converts.

MATT 5:16 - *"Let your light so shine before men that they may see your good works and glorify your Father in heaven."* **NKJV-OB**

In actuality, Jesus was saying that His actions spoke louder than John's words. It is universally true across cultures that the actions in the life of an individual give more credibility to their message than their speaking. An old Fijian proverb, for example, states that *"doing is louder than talking."*

In light of the command "to love our neighbor," we ought to examine what should be the scope of our concern for the neighbors of our community, city, and nation.

1) What has been our own individual concern for the poor and needy

2) What has been our participation as citizens in the community life of our city, state, and nation?

CHAPTER TWO: *PROCLAMATION OR DEMONSTRATION OR...?*

GOD'S I.D. WITH THE POOR

Scripture is replete with testimony of God's identification with the poor. While there is the strong need to know God, we ought to reflect on what it actually means to know Him. "Knowing" God, according to Jeremiah, is to be concerned for the needs of the people around us.

JER 22:16 – *"He defended the cause of the poor and needy, and so all went well. Is that not what it means to know me?" declares the Lord."* NIV

Isaiah says much the same thing in Chapter *58* while including a strong warning. Isaiah's summation is that if we are not concerned about the needs of people around us, God won't even listen to our prayers. In its passage on the true fast, God tells the Israelites the kind of worship He wants from them is to reach out to the needs of the people around them. Without caring for the poor and needy, He says we miss the mark.

Paul as the original evangelist and great church planter says that having concern for the poor and needy was the one thing he was "eager" to do.

GAL 2:9-10 - *"James, Peter and John, those reputed to be pillars, gave me and Barnabas the right hand of fellowship when they recognized the grace given to me. They agreed that we should go to the Gentiles, and they to the Jews. All they asked was that we should continue to remember the poo r the very thing I was eager to do."* NIV

Paul found that caring for the needs of the poor was a necessary component of his ministry. There was never any controversy in his heart over the issue.

SCHOOLS OF THOUGHT IN HELPING THE POOR

People will endeavor to help the poor for various reasons and motives.

1) FOR PERSONAL BENEFIT - Sometimes helping the poor is done to ease one's guilt. Being uncomfortable while witnessing the disadvantages of others disturbs our consciences as we enjoy certain levels of comfort and affluence.

Similarly, we may want to do something for God so that He will do something for us. Our help does not necessarily proceed from an attitude of love but as an investment hoping for an ultimate reward from the Lord. This makes our service somewhat mercenary.

Surprisingly, Scripture does not seem to contradict any of these motives. Scripture suggests that most reasons are acceptable. God does not seem to be as particular as one might think when it comes to helping the poor as long as we make the effort to do so. Some mentioned Scriptural motives for helping others are:

Love ....I COR 13, JOHN 14:15, 21
Confirms our Faith ......JAS 2:17-26, I COR 9:22
Compassion...............MATT 14:14
Sympathy..................HEB 10:34
Mercy........................LUKE 6:35
Reward......................LUKE 6:36-38
Approval....................MATT 25:14-30
Glorify the Lord...........MATT 5:16
To Win Others............I COR 9:22

2) LIBERALISM - Back in the 1850s, a liberal theology was being espoused which taught that the Kingdom of God could be ushered in and that the return of Jesus to earth could be hastened by curing society's ills. Society's ills, such as child labor, poor working conditions, and low wages were mounting due to the abuses and injustices of the accelerating industrial revolution.

The Church robustly plunged into attempts to remedy some of these growing injustices by striving to meet the social and physical needs of the people. Soup kitchens, homeless shelters, and such things as the temperance movement arose to counteract these growing menaces to society, especially in the industrial nations. This great thrust toward social activism of the Church became known as the "S*ocial Gospel.*" Feeling hard-pressed by the urgency of these growing evils, there arose an overemphasis in the Church to people's physical and social needs to the detriment and neglect of the spiritual ones.

At its extreme, this social activism conveyed the notion that one could save oneself and society through acts of justice, mercy or, as the Bible calls them, "good works." Works became the road to salvation. But we know this isn't true. It's clear that salvation is a free gift.

EPHE 2:8 - *"For it is by grace you have been saved, through faith--and this not from yourselves, it is the gift of God, not by works so that no one can boast."* NIV

JAMES 2:17 - *"...faith by itself, if it does not have works, is dead."* **NKJV-OB**

Works in no way merit our salvation; rather works are the evidence of it. As stated earlier, it is an outflow of loving God, a process that occurs when we came to the point of passing from non-believer to believer.
(MATT 25 does suggest, however, that unless we get the principle right on loving our neighbor, salvation will not be possible.)

In this mind-set, at its extreme, we often do not sense the urgency to minister to the spiritual condition of the poor. In effect, we become irresponsible Christians by ultimately not addressing people's spiritual needs as well.

Oftentimes Jesus does not receive the credit and glory for our benevolence. It is not uncommon for the United Nations to employ volunteer Christian agencies for its work and yet attempt to prohibit fulfilling their responsibilities as Christians to share their faith. The United Nations, a humanistic organization, receives the assistance and credit for Christian volunteerism while restraining Christians, serving in the love of God, from sharing their faith and thereby nullifying credit that should go to the Lord.

While working as missionaries in the refugee camps in Thailand, we were under a signed agreement not to actively proselytize among the refugees. In other words, we were forbidden to preach the Gospel, despite our volunteerism. According to proper interpretation, this meant that we could not take the initiative but it did not preclude us from sharing if the refugees freely asked us about our personal beliefs or Christianity. Naturally, we would pray daily that God would open opportunities and lead refugees to us who would be interested enough to initiate the conversation and ask us questions. From time to time, several would ask why we were there working as volunteers in the camps which led to opportunities to share our faith. Through questions from the refugees as to why we would come from a rich country to help them in their misery, we had many opportunities to share about the love of God and our lives as Christians.

With the help of Overseas Missionary Fellowship, a missionary organization in the camps, I was able to obtain literature in the form of comic books depicting the story of the crucifixion and resurrection of Jesus in the Khmer language, the language of the refugees. So as not to violate our agreement with the U.N. by actively distributing the comic books and becoming guilty of proselytizing, I would leave a few of the comic books strewn around our work place on tables and benches. They would mysteriously disappear. Then I would bring more and they would disappear. I began to bring Bible tracts, small pamphlets and other literature and they would all disappear as well.

Eventually, I brought a few New Testaments in the Khmer language and they would disappear, too. Ultimately, the questions arose from the refugees, confounded by our presence as volunteers from an affluent country (especially me with my wife and two children in the camps), working there on their behalf,

"Why are you here? Why are you doing this for us? You come from a rich nation with your family to help us. Why?"

It was then when we had the opportunities to share our faith and testify to the love God had for them and His desire to have them in a relationship with Himself.

****

On a rare occasion, a visiting missions outreach team from Hong Kong, composed of several international members, came to our work site. I thought it would be a nice treat for my refugee workers to have a break from their work duties of making the water jars for water storage for the rest of the refugees in the camps and see and hear a little creative art-type ministry as offered by the team. I explained their presence to the refugees and that what they did was Christian-oriented. The refugees were eager for the presentation.

The FEET (Far East Evangelism Team as they were called) were not officially camp workers but only visitors there for the day. Their ministry to us was simple; they sang a few choruses, performed some small dance numbers and gave some short personal testimonies, all in the confines and shade of our thatched-roof-bamboo shelter.

Much to my surprise, one of their team, Gwen, gently asked the refugees that if there were any that wanted to become Christians and have "Jesus to come into their heart" they should raise their hands. All 50 of my workers raised their hands.

Inasmuch as most of the refugees were from communal type cultures, they were apt to respond all together in a communal type fashion. To guard against what might have been that type of 100 % communal response (or believing possibly there was something misunderstood inasmuch as it is rare that every single person in the group would respond positively) I repeated the invitation. Again, every man responded positively. Perplexed, I gave another invitation for them to kneel down this time to see if they were really sincere, thinking perhaps that would separate out the insincere ones. All knelt down. We closed our session and ended our workday. Still feeling full of unrest and not entirely satisfied at the 100 % response of my workers, the next day I pushed the issue further and asked for those who were really serious about their willingness to become Christians to come to a Bible study after work the following day. Thirty-six workers came.

I felt we now had our true number of positive respondents. Thirty- six of my fifty refugee workers had come to the Lord, and we were not allowed preach the Gospel. Written agreements could not stop the promise of MATT 5:16 at work.

3) FUNDAMENTALISM - Fundamentalists will claim from experience that as social and physical concerns of the Church increase, zeal for spiritual concerns diminishes. Historically, they say, as we've concerned ourselves with social issues and the needs of those around us, we have lost our spiritual cutting edge and our fervor for evangelism. They consider this too great a price to pay.

In reaction to the trends of the social gospel, fundamentalists and some Pentecostals pressed harder to advance the message for individual, spiritual salvation through regeneration and not works. The social gospel they claimed was bordering on heresy.

To avoid contamination by this so-called "heresy" and to preserve their own integrity, the fundamentalist, evangelical movement began to avoid social involvement. At its extreme, it began to treat the Great Commandment, to love our neighbor, as a suggestion and relegated it to a secondary level of importance requiring its obedience only when convenient. It would rationalize that the souls of people were more important and since we just have so much money, people, and resources to go around, we need to get on with the job of saving souls. In the ensuing years, "works" were often neglected. Thus, fundamentalists came very near to falling into heresy of their own.

While leading an outreach team during the Korean Olympics in 1988 at Seoul I came upon a boy lying face down on a stairway platform leading down to the underground trains. We had just finished an open-air outreach and were heading back to our housing venue. When I came upon the boy, I was horrified and so dragged him to the sidewall out of the way of foot traffic to keep the hundreds of people going up and down the stairway from having to walk over him and around him. I didn't know if he was drunk, on drugs, or was medically in distress. The rest of my team that had gone on ahead came back looking for me because of my delay, thinking I was lost. While still kneeling beside the boy I looked up into their faces and all at once realized, " My goodness, they had passed him by too."

All of us paid our own expenses and made great sacrifices to be on that outreach.

We had just preached the Gospel in the park to hundreds of university students and yet for whatever reason, whether to keep the time schedule, fatigue or whatever, our team had walked over that young man lying on the platform just like everyone else. It was almost like the downside of the Samaritan story being re-enacted all over again. Had we totally neglected that boy, we could very well have missed the opportunity to make a statement into the spiritual realm by that great omission.

We become confused as to which is the more important of the two great commands when, in fact, what is really confusing us is our failure to distinguish between the "ends" and the "means" of preaching the Gospel.

There is no question that the regeneration of a soul is God's highest intention. That's the "ends." But we act and carry out evangelism as if "preaching" is the "ends." Preaching can only be considered a "means." It is only one of the " means" of communicating the Gospel, not the exclusive one. Demonstrating the Gospel is another.

Often our preaching is amiss. We preach a message "that God loves you," therefore come to God." "Come to Jesus because Jesus loves you." This can lead to feeble conversions resulting in shallow commitments or woeful backsliding. The message we're meant to preach is that people can be forgiven for their sins. That's the Good News. There is forgiveness for our sins, but we need to believe in Jesus and repent.

In effect, we preach the love of God that ought to be demonstrated and rarely preach the call to repentance. Demonstrating the love of God fortifies the call to repentance.

It's rational to believe that the Great Commission is being impaired while the Great Love Commandment goes unfulfilled. We might even suggest that the way to fulfill the Great Commission is to obey the Great Commandment. The whole disjointed world is waiting for a demonstration of the love of God.

Years ago, when lecturing at a Bible college in Australia, I learned of their street ministry in which the students drove in vans through sectors of the city picking up homeless, drunks, drug addicts, and runaways to put them in touch with various government agencies already designed and prepared to help. Because of that, the Bible students gained a citywide reputation for public service. Many of the students had been invited by city officials to go into some of the public high schools to teach religion and Bible classes.

By facilitating and serving their community, they demonstrated the love of God and impacted the society around them to such a degree that it led to even greater areas of influence through the public school system.

Jesus wants us to remember His death. He reckoned that His action on the cross would confirm God's love for us. Validated on the cross, His love would draw men to Himself. Believers, demonstrating the Gospel through their actions, could persuade humanity to become lovers of God as promised in MATT 5:16. Love demonstrated, Jesus confirmed, is the weightier testimony. Proclamation is best when supported by our actions.

4) MISSION / EVANGELICAL - In this mind-set we use our good works as a way of seeking an entry to preach the Gospel. Perhaps most of us fall in this category. There seems to be nothing intrinsically wrong with this disposition except that in the eyes of the Lord our motives may be considered dubious. We can use good works as a strategy to capture an audience for preaching the Gospel, but we need to be careful that our agenda and methods aren't manipulative. If food, housing, and clothing hand-outs are hiding an agenda to preach the Gospel then we are really flirting with manipulation. If the motivation behind our efforts is not truly love, our motivation can be discernible to the very non-believer we are trying to reach. We can provoke cynicism in the non-believer instead of the real response for which we're hoping.

Classically, if our good works are a sincere demonstration of the love of God, the non-believer will eventually ask the question, *"Why are you doing this?"* and the door will be opened to share our faith with a heart prepared to listen.

(We acknowledge that a motivation of love is not just within the exclusive domain of demonstrators of the Gospel as such, since our preaching and evangelism surely can be motivated by love. Paul, the evangelist, said that it was the love of God that constrained him to preach the Gospel. We want to affirm that it is love shed abroad in the hearts of believers that impels them to traverse rivers, valleys, mountains, or jungles often under great hardship to preach the Gospel to a hidden people group, no less than another laying down one's life for a leper.) We do maintain that, to the non-believer, our efforts may not be easily perceived as love, as much as love demonstrated through caring and practical helps along with our preaching.

5) HOLISTIC - Somehow within us there needs to be an integration of the concepts of *Proclamation* and *Demonstration*. Jesus wasn't dichotomized. Both ministries flowed out of His nature. If we profess to be followers of Jesus, then it ought to be our nature to be sharing our faith and loving our neighbor as the occasion arises. Because someone prefers to do evangelism and feels that it is his gifting, that does not exempt him from the command to minister to the practical needs of those around him. Feeling justified in seeking lost souls while being insensitive to their needs is not very loving. Some denominations practice a dichotomy and are given over to one or the other of these two concepts – either demonstration or proclamation. In one denomination, it is actually discouraged to do evangelism or church planting if one is working in the mercy component of their outreach ministry. Conversely, mercy works are discouraged in the evangelism component. One is encouraged to join some other organization if one wants to do both.

We ought to keep in mind that neither the evangelist nor a health care missionary is our model. Jesus is our model. The whole Gospel was embodied in Jesus. Evangelism and mercy ministry aspects were contained in Him in full. He ministered to each need as it arose. If the need was spiritual, he preached or taught. If the need was physical, He ministered to that need.

A DAY IN THE LIFE OF JESUS

MARK 10:46-56

It's worth an attempt to visualize this situation.

"Then they came to Jericho. As Jesus and his disciples, together with a large crowd, were leaving the city, a blind man, Bartimaeus (that is, the Son of Timaeus), was sitting by the roadside begging. When he heard that it was Jesus of Nazareth he began to shout, 'Jesus, Son of David, have mercy on me!' Many rebuked him and told him to be quiet...." **NIV**

Here was a blind man by the roadside begging ....and they rebuked him....and told him to be quiet. Blind Bartimaeus by the roadside, begging ... ***calling on the name of the Lord***... and the followers of Jesus rebuked him ... and told him to be quiet!

(At this point, we ought to pause and reflect on the above passage momentarily.)

What possibly could have been on the disciple's minds?

"C'mon Jesus, the stadium is full! Hurry, Jesus we don't have time for this, we don't want to be late!! Don't keep the crowd waiting, Jesus!!"

"... but he shouted even more, 'Son of David, have mercy on me!' Jesus stopped.. and said, 'Call him.' So they called to the blind man, 'Cheer up! On your feet! He's calling you.' Throwing his cloak aside, he jumped to his feet and came to Jesus. 'What do you want me to do for you?' Jesus asked him. The blind man said, 'Rabbi I want to see.' 'Go,' said Jesus, 'your faith has healed you.' Immediately he received his sight and followed Jesus along the road."

There was no controversy in the heart of Jesus. .... ***Jesus stopped*** .... and ministered to the man's need.

Christians intent on proclamation of the Gospel only, can often appear arrogant and self- righteous. Demonstration only, however, without a concern for the spiritual needs of people is irresponsible. We need the integration of the two by every Christian to be ministering the full-orbed Gospel as Jesus intended.

"DEVELOPMENT IS NOT AN EVENT OR AN EPISODE BUT A PROCESS. THE PROCESS IS MUCH SLOWER AND PAINSTAKING BUT LONG-TERM SUSTAINABLE RESULTS WILL PROVE THE EFFECTIVENESS OF THE APPROACH."

CHAPTER THREE: *AND WHAT OF MATTHEW 5:16?*

In an attempt to test the truth of MATT 5:16, it became our rallying cry for an evangelism outreach that we conducted with a fresh class of Discipleship Training Students.

GIFT OF WATER OUTREACH PROJECT

Rock Castle Crossroads Discipleship Training School - Powhatan, Virginia

Date: July 4th, 1988 - 10:30 a.m. – 4:30pm

Location: Washington Mall in vicinity of Washington Monument, Washington D.C

Participants: 14 Crossroads students plus 2 Powhatan staff persons

Facilitated by: YWAM staff persons from 133 C Street, Washington D.C.

Mission Statement: This outreach was conducted to prove the truth and efficacy of the Scripture verse:

MATT 5:16 - *"Let your light so shine before men that they may see your good works and glorify your Father in heaven."* **NKJV-OB**

The vision was to distribute a drink of cold water free of charge in the name of Jesus to the holiday crowds on Independence Day in the nation's capital on what was to be a festive day of parades and celebrations. Anticipated temperature was to be around 95 degrees. Anticipated crowds were to be in the thousands.

The simplicity of the act of giving a drink of water in the name of Jesus (or as some students preferred - "God loves you.") was to be maintained throughout the outreach without any flair or fanfare. The project was designed to meet a basic felt need for those people at that time and place. The cup of water was to be a quality product - clean, ice cool and pleasing to look at. By agreement of the students, there was to be no overt preaching, handing out literature or any other form of proselytizing. The act of giving a drink of water in Jesus' name was to be the only "planned" activity.

Equipment Required:

2 portable folding tables

3 large water coolers with taps (1 @ 10 gals. & 2 @ 5 gals.)

2 folding chairs

2000 paper cups

2 water coolers for water carrier replenishments

2 food chests as ice carriers

Large garbage can for discarded cups and trash.

Paper towels

Directional signs with pointers on the walkways and at the serving tables ➡ FREE Ice Water

One sign on the tables stating "This water is provided in the name of Jesus." Small pieces of literature and Bible tracts were placed on the tables for free taking.

Additional Planning and Facilitation:

The whole outreach was under-girded in prayer.

There was great unity and enthusiasm in the team although many had never been involved in any kind of outreach before.

Skilled facilitation was exercised in obtaining required park permits, choosing a location close to water sources for replenishment, easy access for car drop off, selecting high pedestrian traffic areas, tie-ins with local church and ministry groups, and shade areas for team members on break from the heat and sun.

Team members alternated between serving water and answering questions and offering counsel. At a short distance away, we had some of our team members, one with a trained operatic voice, singing short, familiar hymns to the delight of passersby. Crowds gathered.

It was a very hot day. People who were attending the parades and other activities were coming with heavy thirst. The simple service of a cup of water was warmly and appreciably received. Many inquired as to who we were and why we were doing this. Many were astounded that the service was done free and began to drop coins and dollar bills on the tables in gratitude. We insisted that they keep their money and simply accept the water freely without charge. In keeping with the festive day, we kept the mood and interactions light-heated and fun.

One lady, in particular, very fashionably dressed in a nice top and skirt outfit, with a fine hair style, high heels and fine jewelry, seemed way out of character with the rest of the crowd that were more casually dressed for the occasion. She was in obvious distress from the heat as her face gave signs of real flush. I gave her a cup of the water and told her that Jesus loves her. She quickly drank it down and stood there at the table. She handed me the empty cup and said, "Do you think He loves me enough to give me another one?" Gazing at her with surprise, I gave her another one and said, "He loves you so much, you can have as much as you want. You stay there until you're filled." She handed me her empty cup for still another one which I gave her. After momentarily being distracted from her, then turning back to where she had been standing, she was gone.

Several people who came for water were in casts with broken limbs, on crutches, with walkers or some other infirmities and we volunteered to pray for them which they eagerly accepted. Through one of team members who spoke some Spanish, we were able to put a family from San Salvador that had just been evicted from their apartment and spoke very little English in touch with a local church that promised to minister to their need.

As a delightful consequence of the full range of all our activity, about a dozen people accepted the Lord and became Christians at our tables.

And we did not preach the Gospel.

CHAPTER FOUR: *HELPING THE POOR AND THE BIG "D"*

HELPING THE POOR IS NOT UNIQUELY CHRISTIAN, EVEN HUMANISTS DO IT

Most of us do not want to see human suffering or deprivation. The tendency to want to help those in need seems to be, at least in some measure, within all of us. Thus, much has been done, and for the sake of illustration, we'll examine some of the ways that are often used in trying to help the poor.

1) GIVE AWAYS - Money, Food, Equipment, Fertilizers.
It is amazing that after decades of this kind of activity we have not generally helped the poor to escape their poverty. Missionaries coming back from the field are filled with discouragement over the failure of their efforts to make a dent in the poverty cycles of the people to which they've been ministering. Since giving things to people and doing things for them didn't seem to work in alleviating their poverty, it was decided that what was needed was more control over their situations. To produce better results there arose insistence on better workable solutions to their problems and so we began to promote...

2) PROJECTS and PROGRAMS
We began to bring not only our help but our agendas as well. For stricter accountability to achieve the desired results, we began to impose our solutions onto the people. We imposed farm programs, health clinics, built roadways, and despite all our good intentions, the poor remained largely as poor as they were before. Our success in helping the poor was not nearly keeping pace with our good intentions. So then we reasoned that the way to help the poor was to help them modernize.

3) MODERNIZATION
Through this theory, capital and technical advances were invested at the upper levels of cultures, believing that what was needed was more modern equipment and technology. So we began to give tractors, telephones, computers and all kinds of fancy equipment. It was believed that consumerism and consumption and the resultant benefits of the prosperity would have the effect of flowing through the economy and eventually trickle down to the poor.

New jobs would be created at the bottom which would result from the stimulus of investment at the top. The theory was even called *Top Down -Trickle Down.*

The *Green Revolution* in India was intended to touch the lives of the poorest of the peasant farmers in India through new farming techniques and new understanding in the use of seeds, fertilizers and irrigation. The new scheme did not benefit the targeted poor as planned, but only benefited the already prosperous. Instead of prosperity trickling down, it trickled up. The rich became richer, and the poor became poorer or remained largely as poor as they were before. Worse, we had not appropriately discovered the reason for all these failures. Why had the *Green Revolution* been such a success in India yet did not touch the very poor people it was intended to reach in the process?

It was not a case of any mischief or corruption or any untoward administration. What had not been taken into account was that poor lacked experience and competing skills to take advantage of the benefits intended for them. Often, they were illiterate and so did not have access to the necessary information. They had very little in the way of administrative skills or organization. The ones who benefited from every innovation were the educated and already prosperous and those who already had experience in dealing with programs of the type. In any case, those not so poor were able to take advantage of the new benefits and the poor, mired in their disadvantages, were not.

4) MISSIONS / COMMUNITY DEVELOPMENT

Mission agencies began to suggest that if we were going to help the poor, we would need to help the poor directly. Missionary action sought to work at the very levels of the poor by working in slums, poor neighborhoods, and among the peasant farmers to live life with them. Thus, we entered an era when mission agencies began to work among the poor directly. They still brought in their health clinics, schools, farming education, even equipment and technology and every conceivable strategy in trying to help the poor. Years were spent working at the level of the poor, yet the poor remained largely poor and made little progress toward self-reliance.

All these attempts failed because they did not consider that, in their sincere efforts, they had created pathways to ***Dependency.*** The very people they were intending to help were being fixed into a system wherein agendas and decisions were imposed onto them. The poor would have less of a voice and less of an opportunity to participate in the dynamics of their own development. They would continue on the road of having things done for them or having things given to them. They would surrender, in bits and pieces, their own options, self-esteem, dignity, and inherent creative ability to contribute to their own welfare and the welfare of their community. All our systems created a pattern of ***Dependency***. If people have the opportunity to get something for nothing, especially the poor, the temptation is too great, and they will take it. ***Dependency*** is a trap. It is a snare that will thwart the people' s initiative to self-reliance.

Thus, for our part collectively, we have been guilty of undermining the latent ability of the poor to make any contribution to their own improvement by our pattern of ***Paternalism.***

The root word for paternalism is the Latin word "Pater" which means "Father." ***Paternalism*** is that ministry to the poor in which we act and behave as the big, benevolent, all knowing, all generous, all problem solving "Father." If we truly have been acting like the great, big, benevolent, all knowing, all problem-solving Father, how must we have been treating the people? ....*Like children!*

We have been treating them as if they were unable to function and develop on their own except with our ideas, programs, money, resources, and advice. We have acted as if the poor had no abilities, no ideas, or aspirations of their own. In our misguided compassion, we have actually hindered and even thwarted their ability to do things for themselves. We depleted them of their own sense of value and worth along the way. In our faulty sense of generosity, we have treated them as if they were inadequate, or inferior. In overbearing fashion, we imposed our goods, decisions, agendas, and our will unto them.

Dependency in general terms, usually develops on money, advice, counsel, technology and equipment. Moving the poor too quickly toward more sophisticated technology can be futile since the poor may be unable to duplicate or maintain the technology by themselves because of lack of parts and training. Moreover, usually there is not enough technology and equipment to go around so only a few benefit, while the others fall behind. All our efforts should be designed to help the whole community not just a few.

The greatest difficulty with the introduction of technology often is that it is too advanced or sophisticated to fit local technology patterns. Hi-tech equipment makes the people dependent then on outside sources for replacement, renewal or restoration. ***Dependency*** grows. If people are still using wooden instruments or equipment, they will not be much helped by a quantum leap in the sophistication of new technology. Technology advances should be incremental, often to just a notch higher than what they presently have and accessible enough so that everyone can benefit.

If we were to speculate as to what people would do if there was a shortage of outside resources to fit their dilemmas, our immediate answer would be that the people will look within their own environment and within themselves for the solution to their problems.

On the other hand, if outside help and resources are readily available, we must face the contingency that, despite the looming trap of dependency, the temptation would be too great and the people would be sure to take them. The most hurtful result from this kind of paternalism is damage to the spirit and attitude of self-reliance!

What then is the resultant attitude of people who become dependent and continually have things done for them or given to them? Is it gratitude? Rarely! Appreciation? Perhaps! It is more likely resentment.

It seems inconceivable that while we may be acting out of a merciful and compassionate heart, the resulting attitude of those we have been trying to help is not gratitude but disappointment or resentment. Often too, there can be selfishness and greed resulting in demands for even more free goods and services.

How could such unseemly responses arise out of our kindness and good will? The answer lies in the emotional turmoil that people go through when they know they are becoming dependent. They know the risk that lurks in their future as they recognize they are losing control of their own lives. Knowing their well-being and the control of their lives is in someone else's hands can make them feel vulnerable, insecure, and as victims resulting in discomfort, anxiety, and resentment. The veiled fear of being dominated and controlled in becoming dependent creates the tension and resentment.

Where that tension does not exist is probably due to acquiescence to dependency and a future of under-development. Where the tension is irrational it can result in demands for more, rebellion, and disdain for the system itself. The fact remains that dependent people (even communities and nations) can be anything but grateful. Perhaps now, we've entered into an era of community development understood.

5) COMMUNITY DEVELOPMENT UNDERSTOOD

If we want to see people grow and develop and take charge of their own lives, we need to search for ways to help while hindering dependency, encouraging self-reliance, and entering in without the largess of money, technology, goods and services or even advice.

If our Christianity is going to be relevant to the huge number of needs we're going to face, we must be willing to acquire the skills and strategies to be effective in meeting those needs by stimulating self-reliance without creating dependencies. A major answer lies in the ministry of "*community development*" - people improving the quality of their lives collectively, according to their own hopes, choices, and abilities.

What do we think of when we hear the term Community Development?

Most people would say something like construction, water, sanitation, roads, clinics, schools, parks. Those certainly are components.

The first thing that should come to mind when we read or hear the term community development is that it is ***people***. They are the ones we want to see grow and develop. Projects are vital but incidental mechanisms in the process. ***People developing is community development***.

Programs and projects come and go, and they succeed or fail. The impact we ought to look for is that the people grow and develop to their full potential.

****

PATERNALISM (MERCY MINISTRY) .... IS NOT ALWAYS DETRIMENTAL

To avoid confusion, we need to state at this point that paternalism is not always harmful. There are times when we do give things and do things for people. Jesus said we are to give to the poor, hungry, and thirsty, and clothe the naked.

There are situations when giving things to people and doing things for them is vital. The survival of the people may depend on it. There are many situations, however, when we do give and yet it can be an inappropriate remedy for the need we are trying to solve.

There are times when stimulating development may be the more appropriate response than simply giving things to and doing things for people. Different circumstances dictate when we apply giving and when we encourage development.

In the following *schematic*, we compare the interventions for aiding the poor to select the more appropriate option for their condition. Though people may be under stress and suffering, a one-size-fits-all type of help is not always best.

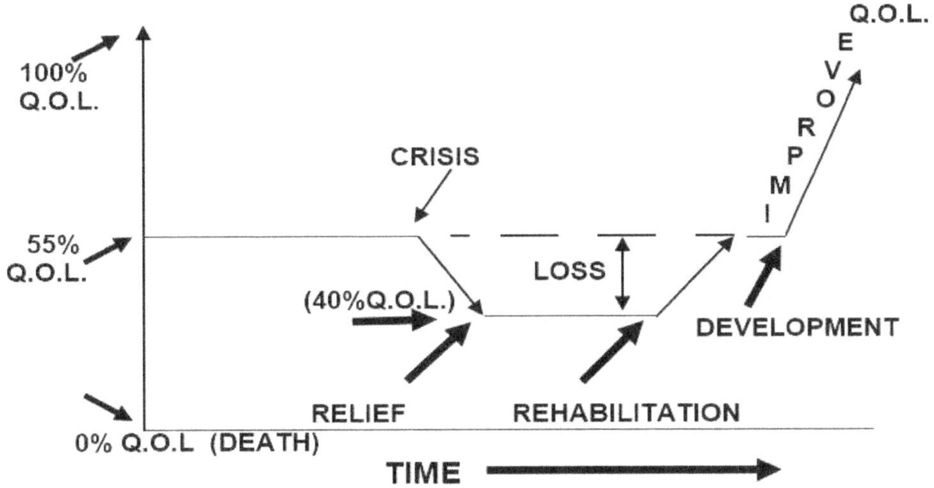

In the above diagram, we hypothetically assume a small village functions in everyday life at a 55 % level Quality-of-Life (Q.O.L.). Only 55 % of their needs are being met. That's 55% of the food, health care, water, literacy, or whatever, that they need for a basic Quality-Of-Life. They are at the subsistence level and it may go on for years.

A ***CRISIS*** arises; perhaps a hurricane or damaging storm devastates their village, of such seriousness that the community's Q.O.L. begins a downward slide. The very survival of the people would be at risk. If there is no intervention it will lead to a Zero ("0") Q.O.L. which would be defined as ultimate elimination or ***DEATH***.

The appropriate intervention for this condition is commonly called ***RELIEF***. It is the situation in which *providers* supply all the needs of the people: shelter, clothing, food, health care, energy. ***PATERNALISM*** is actually required. People in these situations might even be in need of psychological or spiritual counseling. Providers simply give to them and do things for them in this time of vital need. Giving is the only appropriate response.

With a successful intervention, the community settles into ordinary life again. As they proceed through ***TIME***, they function at an even lower Quality-of-Life than before. Now only 40 % of their needs are being met because of their ***LOSS.***

The ***LOSS*** problem is remedied by bringing them back to a point of where they were before. That intervention is called ***REHABILITATION***. The purpose is to bring restoration to the community. An earthquake that does damage to the infrastructure of a community hindering road use, water supply, electrical service or any loss considered temporary and restorable with appropriate action, would fall in this category. Joint action by the victims and temporary outside resources of equipment, materials, and finances is usually the remedy.

REHABILITATION is generally a partnering approach wherein the needy are great contributors to their own recovery. They may require extra equipment or supplies to overcome the devastation they may have suffered. The Mexican recovery from an earthquake years ago was a great example of partnering as the Mexican people supplied the labor needed, while the industrial nations supplied or loaned vast amounts of equipment and know- how.

Though restored, the village is still at that subsistence level of 55% Q.O.L. It is significant that if we continue assisting in *REHABILITATION* through *TIME,* we will risk creating a dependency and the implications of that are not encouraging. If we can lead them to a Quality-of-Life just a notch higher than where they presently are by bringing some improvement, without creating a dependency, that intervention is called *DEVELOPMENT.*

Here is a refined comparison between *RELIEF and DEVELOPMENT* and the various questions they attempt to answer. Using our schematic, we construct a comparison to delineate between the problems, purposes, and strategies which each type of ministry ought rightly to address.

	RELIEF	**DEVELOPMENT**
PROBLEM	CRISIS	POVERTY
PURPOSE	SURVIVAL	IMPROVEMENT
STRATEGY	GIVING	MOTIVATION
AGENT	GIVER	FACILITATOR
RESOURCES	EXTERNAL	INTERNAL
TIME FRAME	SHORT TERM	LONG TERM

A genuine ***CRISIS*** by our definition would be one that is life threatening or a circumstance in which the people have no means of preventing further debilitation or securing their survival. A violent storm that wipes out the entire harvest of a community eliminating their food supply is an example of a crisis.

The proper response to the problem of a ***CRISIS*** is ***RELIEF*** – that of giving things to people and doing things for them. Our *Purpose* in doing so is to ensure the *Survival* of the community.

The problem of *Poverty* and all that poverty entails, wherein needs are not being met but there is no impending crisis or threat to the routine life of the community, is remedied by *Development.* While living at a low Quality-of-Life in a stable condition, the necessary intervention is *Development* to bring lasting improvement to the community. *Development is the answer to Poverty.*

What do we infer from this comparison and what are its implications?

It is evident that *Relief* (giving things and doing things for people) is not the answer to *Poverty! Relief* is the answer to a *Crisis.* It is the appropriate intervention when the survival of the people is at risk.

	RELIEF ← NO!	**DEVELOPMENT**
PROBLEM	CRISIS →	POVERTY
PURPOSE	SURVIVAL	IMPROVEMENT
STRATEGY	GIVING	MOTIVATION
AGENT	GIVER	FACILITATOR
RESOURCES	EXTERNAL	INTERNAL
TIME FRAME	SHORT TERM	LONG TERM

We have not recognized this. We have often been treating the poor through *Relief* schemes, which in so many cases have led them to dependencies.

Development is the proper response to *Poverty* by stimulating people to improve their Quality-of-Life following their own aspirations, hopes, and decisions beginning with their own local resources and skills. The answer to *Poverty* (the needs of the people not being met) is *Development.*

Conversely, *Development* is not the answer to a *Crisis.* It is too slow! If people are without food, they need it now. It is foolish to show them new farming techniques to increase their harvests if they are in immediate hunger and are without food now. The urgency of the *Crisis* demands immediate help. *Relief* is the answer to a *Crisis.*

	RELIEF NO! →	**DEVELOPMENT**
PROBLEM	CRISIS ←	POVERTY
PURPOSE	SURVIVAL	IMPROVEMENT
STRATEGY	GIVING	MOTIVATION
AGENT	GIVER	FACILITATOR
RESOURCES	EXTERNAL	INTERNAL
TIME FRAME	SHORT TERM	LONG TERM

There is frequent confusion over these two approaches that exists even to this day. Agencies, including missions, are ministering *Relief* and fostering dependencies when they should be encouraging self-reliance. Likewise, it's incorrect to stimulate people to fend for themselves while the people are in situations where they are suffering immediate physical needs.

*The strategy in helping people through Relief is the simple act of giving. The strategy for stimulating people toward improvement, development and self-reliance will take some skills in **Motivation.***

To motivate people toward *Development* is to stimulate them to make choices for change and take action on those choices, over which they will feel good about themselves. In addition, the change agents will avoid the mechanisms that lead to dependency but will make every effort to ***Facilitate*** the community toward self-help.

The French word facile means easy. The agent will not be doing things for them or giving things to them but will ***Facilitate*** the poor in a process to do it by themselves.

When the poor can be motivated to assume ownership of the change that's being advanced it is still a great encouragement to them to have access to guidance and counsel while pursuing that change.

Further, the change being advanced ought to require the use of local resources as much as possible, so as not to risk dependency on external sources.
Obtaining materials or supplies from external sources in some cases might be essential. (Communities ought not to have to reinvent the wheel so to speak.) But when obtaining goods or materials from outside sources they ought not to come without some cost to the community so as to inhibit dependency.
Paying, trading or exchanging for goods or supplies from external sources is beneficial since no dependency risk exists. Accepting continual free help from outside sources can be problematic.

For *Time* reference, *Relief* ought to be conducted for short-term duration to avoid the ever-present risk of dependency. The *Crisis,* being what it is, must be overcome, but it is wise to begin motivating the people toward visions of self-reliance, even in their stress, to avoid the shadow of dependency. Allowing notions that *Relief* efforts can go on forever is a trap waiting to disappoint. Needs are too great and resources too few. The poor need to be encouraged to take charge of their own situations.

(There have been situations where outside agencies (churches) have come alongside communities with help by supplying needed but minimal amounts of resources in a kind of development partnership. But this has been where development was already underway in the community and the people were already committed to working toward change and self-reliance on their own. The help provided by the churches was looked on only as supplemental.)

THE VISION OF COMMUNITY DEVELOPMENT

In attempting to stimulate people to help themselves we ought to have clear-cut objectives and know why we are doing it. Doing development work is a powerful method in our aspirations to be obedient to Jesus. It will enhance our possibilities to achieve two main line objectives:

1. to disciple nations through communities by facilitating them through small, strategic activities to improve their Quality-of-Life and growth within the principles of the kingdom of God.
2. to achieve growth in people's attitude and outlook in identifying their own problems and choosing and pursuing their own solutions to those problems.

Such is the call and mission of *Development* work. The language used in the above objectives has been very selectively chosen for content and meaning.

We will make our approach through "***communities***." We will use a bottom-up approach rather than top down. We want the people to grow and develop to their full potential. The people become the most important focal point of all our development efforts. We will not simply endeavor to improve their conditions and environment but seek also to instill the vision of self-reliance toward future outcomes within the community.

Second, we will be "***facilitating***" them through change. We will not be doing it for them or giving it to them but we will maintain a course of action that will make it easy for them to do it by themselves.

We will deliberately choose "***small***" projects initially so as not to risk failure but to achieve a quick success. If we choose large projects that may be too complex or take too long to achieve, the people may get frustrated or discouraged and believe they can't do it. We do not want to reinforce a low image they have of themselves or solidify their own low expectations. A quick success is a necessary component in motivating and encouraging the people and affirming their abilities and potential.

Third, we will address "***strategic***" needs. We cannot meet every need. Oftentimes the needs in the community may be great. We can prioritize and choose the needs we will address through the strategy of planning and choosing what are called the "***felt***" needs.

Planning with the people will help us determine the desirability for change and set priorities according to urgency.

Felt needs are those which are placing continuing stress on the people in some manner, and which are a burden on their backs causing extreme physical hardship or heavy emotional demand. Addressing ***felt*** needs is a serious, meaningful way to improve the Quality-of-Life of the community, one that results in relief and comfort.

Finally, all our activity to bring improvement to their Quality-of-Life ought to be under-girded by using principles of *Kingdom of God.* We will not use bribery, threats, intimidation, coercion or other unseemly methods to stimulate the people in selfish efforts to achieve our goals.

Our second objective would have us look for change in the people's ***attitude*** and ***outlook.*** We ought to have concern about their attitude toward themselves and their outlook in how they view the world. Generally, the attitude of the poor is that they see themselves as incapable or inadequate for improvement and so often simply live in resignation to their plight. Elevating their attitude about themselves is a task which can be accomplished through some motivation principles which we will discuss later.

Growth in their attitude is key for them to take initiative in making choices regarding the problems they face and how to resolve them. The willingness to make decisions for change comes with confidence and the desire to assume ownership of any projected change. It comes with a growing sense of adequacy and self-worth.

Their outlook toward the world may be that the world is a daunting place. They may see it as too overwhelming to make any advances toward their own general welfare.

It has been my peculiar experience to encounter people who were intimidated even by going into stores to shop. The prospect of having so many selections on store shelves created difficult moments for them, making them fear the decision of having to choose the best one.

Starting small in measured steps for a quick success will go a long way to show them that change is possible, and that the world is not such a frightening place. The community will start on the road to development as it begins to identify its own problems and chooses to take actions to solve those problems - their way.

<u>HOW'S IT GOING?</u>

It's important to evaluate from time to time whether we are on track toward our objectives as we work along with the people. Observing certain responses and behaviors that the people exhibit can be evidence of our being on course.

We will know we're making progress if we observe the following:

a) *increased participation by increasing numbers of people in our development initiatives. We want to observe more and more people working together.*

b) *a desire for avoiding or decreasing dependency by the community.*

c) a willingness to use local resources and skills.

d) *an increasing desire for their own decision-making and control.*

CHAPTER FIVE: WHAT'S OUR VIEW OF PEOPLE?

It is easier just to make a donation than to slowly and patiently work through these principles as a change agent with communities toward a long-range greater good. How we view people will be displayed in our interactions with them.

Motivating people to work together and stimulating desire toward self-help while avoiding dependency will require special qualities in a community development practitioner. We ought to reflect on some desirable and expedient qualities necessary in a worker that will help secure more positive outcomes.

In working with communities, cultural sensitivity must be viewed as a given. Being mindful of local customs, norms, and behavior patterns is a necessary commodity. We want to avoid giving offense and creating barriers to cooperative action and successful outcomes with the people.

There are additional qualities helpful in a worker that will enhance one' s potential for success. All of these are based on biblical concepts. Having a greater understanding of these qualities and their application in our daily lives will go a long way to achieving our goals. How we apply them in our work will stem from the overall regard that we have for people in their humanity and their pursuits of happiness. As we have deeper understanding of these concepts and they become operational in our lives, we can hope for greater success in our work

PILLARS OF DEVELOPMENT

1) IMAGE OF GOD

As change agents, we need a deeper revelation of what it means to be made in the image of God.

The biblical narrative reveals that we mortals are made in His image. The significance and implications of that are enormous. Being made in the image of God is what gives us humans our value, dignity and worth. It is a testimony to the fact that we are not simply products of chance with no more value than a collection of fish eggs but that we are imbued with value and worth of the highest order.

No matter how humble our origins, how deprived our circumstances, how weak, feeble, or uneducated we are, we have value and dignity and worth because we are made in the image of God.

Our value is not derived from our family status, credentials, degrees or societal connections and is not dependent on wealth, beauty, intellectual or physical prowess, but on the fact that we are made in His image. No pressure, affliction, or personal calamity can refute that fact. We are made in His image, and it is indestructible.

We may abuse ourselves with alcohol, drugs, or waste our lives and squander opportunities, but that does not alter our value. Others may look down on us, criticize and reject us, but our value cannot be lessened. Our worth is infinite because it comes from God. Some theologians might claim that the image of God in man is blurred or tarnished because of man's propensity for all sorts of depravity. But Scripture declares that the gifts and callings of God are without repentance and thus the image of God in man is permanent.

With that view of ourselves in mind, can we consider that others are made in His image as well? Can we welcome the significance in our interactions and relationships with others as we realize their value, dignity and worth? Can we look a man lying in a gutter, who smells of urine, sweat, and vomit, and insist that he is made in the image of God? Or a beggar in ragged clothes, unwashed, unkempt and believe that he is made in God's image? Can we believe that a streetwalker, in painted face, immodest dress, and in search of a client is made in the image of God? How about the tattooed punker shrieking obscenities in your face as you gently try to share the Gospel message? Maybe he has poured his drink all over you. Can you look at him and believe he is made in the image of God?

We need a deeper revelation of what it means to be made in God's image. God could hold us accountable for our neglect of the poor for no more reason than this - that they are made in His image.

I was raised in a traditional denomination and had the impression that the reason murder was a crime as explicitly forbidden by the 6th Commandment was that the injustice to the slain victim was much akin to stealing away his life. Because we had not given that life, we had no right to take it away. The logic, as I understood it, was that taking that life, murder, was as a sin of stealing. Genesis 9:6, however, clearly points out that the reason murder is a sin deserving of capital punishment is that the victim was made in the image of God. The perpetrator must forfeit his own life since, by his own volition and actions, he has shown an ultimate disregard for the value of the image of God in the victim, and therefore discounts and forfeits his own.

So as community development workers, the revelation that every person is made in the image of God ought to move us to believe in the worth, dignity, and value of others, no matter what their circumstances.

2) THE BODY

For Christians, the metaphorical term "Body of Christ" refers to the universal body of believers in Jesus of which He is the head. It is that total community of believers that make up the universal *"Church"* over which He is recognized as Lord. On the local level, it is a *Body* in which Christians commit to be participants in various kinds of worship, fellowship, and service.

What is significant about the believers that make up the *Body* is that they are endowed somehow with special and unique giftings that are meant to be utilized for the successful operation of the church and the common good of all believers. As believers don't participate in the life of the Church, they cause a type of deficit of their unique gifting which is intended to contribute to the successful operation of the Church.

We borrow the use of the term here as a metaphor to describe the Body of people living together in community who share common culture, services, institutions, hopes, aspirations and stresses. Hence, for our purposes, we liken the term "The Body," to that totality of residents that make up the community.

In the Church, everyone has a role to play, and everyone has a gifting to use for the successful functioning of it. The same principle by faith can be applied to any poor community in the prospects for its development. Can we believe that God, in His great, merciful, and compassionate heart, has somehow invested the necessary essentials, yet untapped, within communities to bring about their improvement? It is plausible. It is well within the framework of God's character to supply support even for non-believers. We not only ought to believe in this principle but trust in it. Does the Lord send rain and sunshine on the unjust as well as the just?

If we are willing to trust in the great grace of God that in any poor neighborhood, slum, remote village, or hill tribe, He has deposited somehow within that community the necessary means and resources to lead to their improvement, we will begin to build a vision of hope. It becomes a hedge against dependency.

Too often, we look to outside resources and relief for our starting point and invite the trend of dependency instead of looking to God.

For development purposes, if we would commit to a greater belief in the concept of the "BODY" as it pertains to communities and their common good, we would enter into a whole new realm of possibilities for helping the poor to help themselves.

This borrowed Body concept, along with knowledge of God's character and providence can help us believe and trust in His provision for the resources, skills and competencies right within communities to bring about their enhanced Quality-of-Life.

In the Thai refugee camps for Cambodians, I was responsible for directing a huge water jar making project for the UN. We employed about 50 refugee workers who were paid a small stipend. For cost cutting purposes, the UN did not want to purchase the jars but wanted us to manufacture them with the raw materials of mortar and cement. They were to be of about 60 gallon capacity and used by each refugee family for the collection and storage of rainwater during the rainy season. Water carted in by tanker was costing the UN roughly one thousand dollars a day for the needs of about 30,000 refugees. Any method to conserve or collect water was employed. The project was difficult since neither the refugees nor I had any experience in making the jars. With the help of World Vision-Australia brochures and training materials, all of us on the project in a step-by-step process set about to manufacture roughly 2,000 water jars. We started with the manufacture of the molds and then casting the water jars in the mortar and cement.

Water jar Photo from World Vision Australia brochure by Rus Alit. Used by permission

The refugees considered it a humanitarian project in which they took great pride for their involvement. They worked with incredible diligence and workmanship.

After the project was well underway and many jars were manufactured and already delivered to various refugee huts, the UN insisted that we make lids for the jars to protect the water from contamination and especially from malaria producing mosquito infestation. That announcement set us back.

We were to produce the lids from the raw materials of tin with tools that were supplied. The tin came in 4 ft. by 8 ft. sheets. As before, none of us had a clue as to how to work with tin, let alone form it and shape it for lids. To me, this became a heavy burden and a matter of considerable stress. I had to call on my only resource and so I began to pray. I asked the Lord to show me the way to success on the lids.

After a few days, a refugee stood in the doorway to our work-site hut awaiting my invitation to come in. He was tall, of military style posture, middle aged, extremely handsome in appearance, with well-groomed, wavy, white-gray hair. If had he been wearing a tie and business style suit one would have guessed he was a banker or some government official. When I asked what he wanted, he said he wanted to work on our project.

From his bearing and appearance, I could not imagine why he would want to work with us. I asked him what he could do and what skills he had. He said, "I'm a tin-smith."

Such is the love and concern for His people of our prayer answering God..

3) ACCEPTANCE

ROM 15:7 - *"Accept one another, then, just as Christ accepted you..."* NIV

Accepting others as they are is especially critical in dealing with poor and undeveloped people. We can make judgments based on their circumstances or deprivation and communicate a paternalism that is detrimental to our relationships and effectiveness. It's worse if we communicate an attitude of low expectations as well. We need a greater revelation of what it means to accept others.

We can communicate and poorly disguise an attitude of superiority. Once we do, it is an impression that is extremely difficult to displace. We can allow critical and judgmental thoughts to lurk in our minds that hold the people condemnable for their sorrowful predicament. Often, too, our acceptance of others is not a true acceptance but a patronizing tolerance with an attendant reserve or even condescension. We ought to have an appreciation and respect for the cultural differences between us.

Our attitude of superiority can be unintended but real and can be prevented by considering the potential of others and viewing them in light of the image of God.

During an open-air evangelistic team outreach at the Korean Olympics in Seoul 1988, I sat with an elderly Korean man who invited me to join him on a park bench. He spoke somewhat good English in addition to his native Korean. He had been a prisoner of war in China during WWII where he learned to speak Chinese. Later he learned to speak English when he was liberated by American soldiers during the latter stages of the war.

After sharing some personal bio, family pictures, and the Gospel with him on the park bench, he graciously invited me to his home for tea. We had a nice visit with small talk and tea and upon taking my leave to rejoin our team; he wanted to give me a gift for remembrance of my visit. He took a paper scroll from a small desk and with black ink and a brush, while sitting on the floor, began drawing Chinese characters on the scroll. He had drawn four large characters on the scroll of paper which was about four feet in length. The Chinese characters represented a beautiful and an interesting piece of artwork. Not knowing what the characters meant I asked him to interpret.

The first character, he said, was patience, the second was tranquility or peace of mind, the third was love, and the fourth was acceptance.

He had my understanding for the first three but mingling them with the concept of "acceptance" was somewhat strange to me. He explained it this way. He wanted to be accepted for who he was because he had value, worth, and dignity as a person. He wanted to be accepted with his cultural background, language, and customs just as he was since, though being different, they were in no way inferior anyone else's. His feelings were reinforced from his experience of having been mistreated as a prisoner of war. He felt so passionately about it that he equated acceptance on the same plane as being loved. To him, being loved and being accepted were of equal importance.

There is enough rejection in this world. Everywhere we turn we can experience rejection. The whole world wants to minister rejection and communicate a message of inferiority and insecurity that we are not lovable or adequate. We're either too small, too tall, too heavy, too skinny, not smart enough, not beautiful enough, not rich enough, not handsome enough, or complexion not of the right sort that we must be rejectable.

Every Christian ought to resolve in their hearts not to minister rejection again. Christians need to be ministers of acceptance and bring healing to those wounded by the negative messages of this world. We need to accept others as Christ has accepted us. They are lovable and acceptable.

During that Korean outreach, the organizers of the outreach had assigned two young Korean women to each of our teams to act as facilitators. They were to act as our translators, our guides, facilitate us to and from outreach venues, help us navigate the various transport systems, assist us in ordering meals, and generally look after our welfare in their city.

Wisely, because of the potential difficulties in working with our female, cross - cultural friends, the organizers advised all our teams to do what we could to treat them as an integral part of our teams. They would not simply be our facilitators and functional guides; we were to treat them as one of us.

We took the advice seriously and did what we could to integrate them and embrace them as full members of our team. When we took meals or went for drinks, they came with us and we paid for their selections out of our team funds. We did the same for transport costs. In every way we knew how, we attempted to treat them as one of us and members of our teams.

We saw a lot happen on that outreach. People came to the Lord at railway stations, in parks and on buses and trains. We saw people miraculously healed, weeping with repentance in the streets, looking for Bible tracts, and gathering by the hundreds to hear a Gospel message.

I believe none of it would have been possible without the tremendous unity that was engendered on our team. The unity was derived from the spirit of love and acceptance that we had shown to one another.

When we were departing to return to the States, in our farewells, our two facilitators remarked how much they appreciated being treated with such respect and as equals by our teams.

4) HUMILITY (LEARNER)

Reciprocal relationships – Willing to receive from others – Deferring to one another.

PHIL 2:3 - *"...consider others better than yourselves."* **NIV**

We need a greater revelation of what it means to be humble. As our title suggests it is synonymous with willingness to learn or receive from others. It is a willingness to respect other's viewpoints and way of doing things.

When our family worked in the refugee camps in Thailand, which were under United Nations jurisdiction and control, we were not allowed to live in the camps and so we had to maintain living quarters outside in a nearby Thai village.

When working in the camp, we had been wisely cautioned by our team leaders not to eat with the refugees. We were never sure how the refugees handled their food in those situations with poor storage and no refrigeration capabilities. In order to maintain our health priorities and avoid sickness so as not to become a burden on the rest on the team, we were strongly advised not to eat with them. Intestinal sicknesses were common in the camps and contracting dysentery, or an amoebic illness was not rare.

On one occasion, however, a refugee couple invited my wife and me to their housing for an evening meal. We wanted to be obedient to our leader's advice not to eat with the refugees, yet sensitive to the request of the inviting couple. We felt somewhat uncomfortable in simply turning them down as they were willing to share what little food and provision they had with us.

It was a humble invitation, but we wanted to do the right thing. In consulting our leaders, they left it up to us and suggested that we pray about the whole situation. We submitted it to the Lord in prayer and felt released to accept the invitation.

We had the meal virtually in the dark, except for some small candlelight, with the couple and their four children. Quietly, Ursula and I prayed over the food so that the Lord would keep us from getting sick. The meal was rice- water soup (simply water with rice in it, flavored with chicken feet) and some veggies. We also had water to drink, which should have been a real no-no, but we trusted God to keep us safe.

Following the meal during the course of the evening, we learned that the father of the family had been a professor of nuclear physics with a PhD. degree at a university in Cambodia. His frail, gentle and accommodating wife, in her plain and simple dress, with plain, straight hair drawn back, and a tooth missing in front, looked very sad and forlorn. She was a medical doctor – a pediatrician.

This couple, in the dire circumstances of the refugee camps, hosted us with their meager provisions and hospitality. God was teaching us a deep lesson in humility.

We could have turned down their invitation simply as being inadvisable on the basis of their poor and wretched circumstances. We could have dismissed the whole idea with any excuse and never have learned from their personal experiences. Worse, we would never have learned of the skills and giftings that were deposited in that couple which we could have completely overlooked.

We need to have the humility to be learners and believe that no matter how backward or deprived the people are to whom the Lord is sending us, we have something to learn from them. All peoples have skills, giftings and experiences from which we can learn. We need to have the readiness and willingness to learn from them. If we act as if we have all the answers and we' re the only source of knowledge in our way doing things, we will initiate a one-way relationship, generate dependency and damage our attempts at promoting development. We need to have a two-way, reciprocal relationship, acting as receivers as well as bringers.

WHAT'S WRONG WITH THIS PICTURE?? [3]

5] SERVANTHOOD

Another concept we need a greater understanding of is that of servanthood. We need a deeper revelation of what it means to serve others.

I have heard people use the term, sometimes rather glibly, but conceptually hardly ever explaining what servanthood really means. Is it something like fetching someone's newspaper or slippers, washing their car, or cleaning their room? What does it really mean to serve somebody in a practical sense? How is servanthood worked out in our personal relationships and interactions? I never really had a clear understanding of what "serving others" really meant. Then I heard a speaker by the name of Jack Winter[4] give this definition. He said simply:

"You can know if you have a servant's heart, if you want to see others successful."

The implications in this concept are enormous. Do you want to see others successful? Are you willing to work at it? Jesus said it flatly, that He came to serve and not be served. LUKE 22:27 - *"...I am among you as one who serves."* ***NIV***
If we were to work for each other's success, we would not have to be concerned about our own success or advancement. Others would be concerned about our successes for us, while we, likewise, would be concerned and working for their success.

3 John Steward, The Gift That Releases (Australia: World Vision, artist unknown, 1994) p.12

4 Jack Winter (1931-2002) co-founder of Daystar Ministries, St. Louis Park, Minnesota

If all of us were to work to see each other successful in fulfilling our destiny in God, what would that do for the Church and Body of believers? What if we could overcome our own petty jealousies, ambitions, and desires to receive praise, credit, and promotion?

PHIL 2:4 - *"Each of you should look not only to your own interests but also to the interests of others."* NIV

We can only imagine the unity and power in which we would move as a body of believers. If followers would work to see their leaders successful in the roles and callings that God has for them; while conversely leaders would be working to see their followers fulfill the roles and callings God has for them, we would move in such power and unity to advance the Kingdom of God. The world, mired in the competition, jealousy, selfishness, and ambition to which it is accustomed, would take notice.

While Ursula and I directed a ministry center in Guam, one of the ministries we conducted was a small discipleship training school. It was an in-residence program comprising a lecture phase and an outreach phase for practical fieldwork.

Two young Guamanians came calling at our house requesting admission to our coming DTS. The younger boy, about 18 years old, seemed to be the leader of the two. He appeared more confident, articulate, talkative, and assertive. He was a prime candidate for the school. His companion, though 25 years old, seemed to be more shy, hesitant, and passive with something of a plump physique. He would hardly lift his eyes so as to avoid making eye contact when speaking, while scuffing swingingly at the floor with his feet in a kind of timidity as he hesitated and struggled with his words.

Whereas younger Francisco could easily qualify for our coming school, we suggested to the shy Roberto that with a little preparation and mentoring he could easily qualify for our future DTS. But to our surprise, Roberto took a stand. He said he had just come to know the Lord and didn't want to wait but wanted to know more about God. He had heard about our school and was eager to enroll. Because of his earnestness, my wife and I decided to pray over his application and eventually felt assured to accept him in the school.

During the course of the DTS, while sharing some personal testimony, he testified that when he was about thirteen years old, his father came to him and said, "Roberto, you're not really my son. You're mother had been playing around with other men when we were younger and you are result of one of those relationships but you're really not my son."

One can only imagine the immediate, crushing devastation and rejection Roberto felt, particularly in the island culture where family bonds are powerful forces even down through extended family relationships. All at once, Roberto felt like he didn't belong and that his life was a fraud and a deception.

Among other things, he further testified that when his "father" wanted to discipline him he would hit him across the back and legs with a 2 by 4 piece of lumber or burn cigarette butts in his skin to punish him.

He related how the pain of rejection at the time was so great he regressed psychologically and began to suck his thumb like a baby. Now, some twelve years later with a hunger to know God, he was in our missionary training school.

Following the classroom phase of the DTS, that team went on a two-month practical outreach to the Philippine Islands. Facilitated by a local training center in Manila, the Guam team moved into the squatter zone on the massive garbage dump among the dwellers who were scratching out a living by scavenging among the refuse and garbage for usable and saleable items. This created something of a stir within the Pacific region as news spread that the Guam team had moved in among the squatters on the garbage dump. Roberto was on that team.

Following the outreach and the return to Guam, Roberto expressed a desire to become a permanent part of our team and staff.

I began to work with him and mentor him in small ways. I loaned him my Bible commentaries and study books. I mentored him in work habits and personal character attributes. When attending association meetings with other pastors and missionaries, I took him along to observe and experience associating with notable people in ministry. I wanted to him to feel a confidence.

Many home church pastors on the island often sought the help of our staff with the ministries in their churches. They would often call for team members to assist with youth groups, worship teams, Sunday school or discipleship programs. They would often request Steve, Kevin or Marlene to come and help.

After a time, when pastors called, I began to suggest that they would need to take Roberto. After their hesitant remarks that they didn't want Roberto and my refusal to send anyone else, they would eventually consent to take Roberto. Over time, eventually the calls started coming in, "Would you please send us Roberto!"

There came the time when my wife and I were to leave Guam and relinquish the leadership to others. Before we left, the Catholic churches on Guam were having a major annual youth rally for 600 of the top Catholic youth of Guam. The Catholic schools on Guam were excellent schools that attracted students from the other islands and even as far away as the Philippines.

It was a major event for the Catholic youth with many clergy attending and Roberto. . .was a featured speaker. He challenged them to a relationship with Jesus Christ.

Do you want to see others successful? Are you willing to work at it so that they might attain their full potential and destiny in God? We need a greater revelation of what it means to serve others. Seeing others successful, and to be willing to work at it!

CHAPTER SIX: *YOU DON'T SAY?*

The following are reprints of bulletins and pamphlets circulated widely during the 1980s in and around the Solomon Islands. The Solomon Island Development Trust was probably responsible for these circulars but the circumstances, the authors and their whereabouts especially of Mr. Henry T. Samani are unknown. The late Dr. John Roughan and Abraham Beanasia were perhaps the overseers of the use and circulation of these hand-outs.

We apologize for the low-grade quality of the reprints. We thank Dr. Alastair McIntosh[5] , for his advisement in the use of these materials.

They are incorporated here to give the reader some acquaintance with the views of local agencies and development workers on these subjects at that time and place.

5 Dr. Alastair McIntosh, founder and director of GalGael Trust, Glasgow, Scoland. http://www.alastairmcintosh.com/

WHAT IS COMMUNITY DEVELOPMENT?

by Henry T Samani

Community development has to do with change - change in the way of life of people. It is not about change to one person as she or he gets older. It is about change in the lifestyle of a group of people.

Talking about community development is not to speak of one person just helping himself or herself without worrying what happens to other people. Community development is people working together so that all the people in the group are helped.

A community is a group of people who feel they belong together, who see each other from day to day and who can work together as a group.

The word "development" is not a clear word. Some people speak about development all the time. They think it is a good thing. But when you ask them what they mean, they are not sure. Development is about change in the way of life of the people. Development usually means change with growth.

Community development is therefore about social change and growing. But what kind of change and what kind of growing?

Kinds of development

Self-determination begins with the "felt needs" of the community. It fits in with the culture of the people. It means that people themselves participate in deciding and doing what is needed. Self-determination is when people themselves are in control. The people decide for themselves what is good. The people decide who will do it, what time and how it will be done.

In *small development*, ordinary people do something themselves to improve their way of life. A family may learn to keep chickens. Or people grow new kinds of food for themselves or to sell. In small development there is change, but the ordinary people control it and they get something good out of it for themselves. There may be money from outside to help the people get started. There may be outside advisers to help the people grow better food or show them how to build better houses. People must produce everything they need themselves.

In *agency development* changes are brought about by someone outside (government departments, churches and non-government organisations) to try to help the people in a community. Often the agency people have the idea and don't find out what the people are really thinking. Someone from the agency might make a flying visit to get the people to agree, and fail to listen to the people if they have a different idea.

In agency development there is change which is supposed to be for the good of the people, but the people do not have any real say or control. Many things that happen in our communities are done for people by outside agencies, such as the "development" that went on in mission stations. The white missionaries decided what should happen. This is what we call agency development.

Sometimes, though, the skills and knowledge of outside agencies may benefit local people and villages. However, the help agencies give must be for what local people and villages decide they need.

The decision for outside help to come into the village must be made by the village in full understanding of how the help will fit with the pattern of village life. It is best if outside help is agreed upon by the village only in cases where the villagers cannot achieve something by doing it themselves.

Big development means big projects which cost big money. Many white people like big development because there are more jobs and big money. But care must be taken with big development, because it destroys the land, rivers and animals, as logging companies often do. Sometimes the most important things in life are lost through big development.

There are often problems for villages from big development. Big development often sees the creation of wage jobs as important. However, where people are working full time for wages there is little time left for them to undertake communal tasks in the village and tend their gardens.

While villages often have a need for money it is best that it comes from small projects which fit with other tasks of village life. Before villages agree to projects which offer full time wage jobs they must weigh up carefully the merits of each proposal and the problems it will create for the village. Big development often creates wage jobs for only a small number of people in an area while using much of the forest, the land and the fish in the sea. Intelligent small development, where new skills are used wisely, can provide cash income for many while not using up the good things which the land and the sea give.

VQLI - VILLAGE QUALITY OF LIFE INDEX

VILLAGE ____________

DATE ____________

VILLAGE LEVEL		FAMILY LEVEL		TOTAL
(ADULT WELL-BEING)				
		housing	(15) ___	
		a) off ground		
[illegible]	(10) ___	b) cleaned daily		
rubbish removal	(10) ___	c) no holes		
sanitation	(15) ___	kitchen	(10) ___	
		a) stove		
	÷ ___	b) food table	÷ ___	
		c) cook pots		
water supply	(15) ___	d) eating things		
bush line	(10) ___	personal goods	(10) ___	
animals	(05) ___	a) clothing		
		b) bed		
		c) cleaning material		___
		d) box/cases		
(CHILD WELL-BEING)				
Health Committee	(15) ___	mosquito net	(5) ___	
Health Education	(15) ___	first aid box	(5) ___	
	÷ ___	bedding	(5) ___ ÷ ___	
		clothing	(5) ___	
Transportation	(15) ___	plates	(5) ___	___
Medical Box	(05) ___	torch/lamp	(5) ___	
Health Aid	(10) ___	desk/study	(10) ___	
(COMMUNAL WELL-BEING)				
ORGANIZATION		personal tools		
		a) garden tools	(15) ___	
meeting place	(15) ___	b) house tools		
budget	(10) ___	c) hunting and fishing tools		
	÷ ___		÷ ___	___
education	(15) ___	garden	(20) ___	
tools	(10) ___	chickens, pigs, ducks	(15) ___	
REMARKS			÷ 3 ___	
			SCORE ___	
		NUMBER OF PARTICIPANTS ___		

The Village Quality of Life Index enables communities to assess their own stage of development

WATKAEN DEVELOPMENT?

The caption commentaries and drawings modifications are my own, adopted from notes of Dr.Roughan

DISCUSS: WHAT KIND OF DEVELOPMENT?

CHAPTER SEVEN: *WHO SAYS DEVELOPMENT IS AN ANSWER?*

GENESIS NOTES ON DEVELOPMENT:

Oftentimes I'm challenged to provide a biblical basis for my thoughts on development. Many purists claim they can see the call to help the poor in the Scriptures but are unable to find where it speaks of stimulating the poor to help themselves. I've been accused of attempting to avoid my responsibility as a Christian in giving to the poor by suggesting that we ought to move them to help themselves. It's imperative that we present a Scriptural basis for development to justify and undergird our advocacy of stimulating the poor toward self-help.

We'll begin with some reflection on several verses in Genesis:

GEN 1:1-3 - *In the beginning, God created the heavens and the earth. Now the earth was formless and empty, darkness was over the surface of the deep, and the Spirit of God was hovering over the waters. And God said, "Let there be light, and there was light.*

1:6 - *And God said let there be an expanse between the waters to separate water from water.*

1:9 - *And God said, "Let the water under the sky be gathered to one place, and let dry ground appear." And it was so.*

1:11 - *Then God said, "Let the land produce vegetation: seed bearing plants and trees on the land that bear fruit with seed in it, according to their various kinds." And it was so.*

1:14 - *And God said, "Let there be lights in the expanse of the sky to separate the day from the night and let them serve as signs to mark seasons and days and years, and let them be lights in the expanse of the sky to give light on the earth."*

1:20 - *And God said, "Let the water teem with living creatures and let birds fly above the earth across the expanse of the sky."*

1:24 - *And God said," Let the land produce living creatures according to their kinds: livestock, creatures that move along the ground, and wild animals, each according to its kind." And it was so.*

1:26 - *Then God said, "Let us make in Our image, in our likeness, and let them rule over the fish of the sea and the birds of the air, over the livestock, and over all the earth, and over all the creatures that move along the ground."* **NIV**

So is God interested in development?

It says that God began where there was Zero Quality-of-Life. There was darkness; the earth was void and empty. It was formless. No color, no light, nothing. Zero.

Then God gave us Creation: trees, oceans, moons, stars, light, animals, roses, horses, potatoes, kittens, watermelon, coconuts, tomatoes, bananas, whales - all Creation came into being from a Zero Quality-of-Life.

A careful reading of verses 11 and 24 will show us that those are not direct "creative" acts of God but are truly *"developmental"* acts. It says *"out of the ground"* in verse 11, He gave us plants, and trees and fruit-bearing plants. "*Out of the ground"* in verse 24, He gave us animals and crawling things. Even verse 20 might be construed as a developmental act, suggesting that the water produced living creatures. Not all these verses depict direct creative acts but some, in reality, are developmental acts. *God is very interested in development!*

WHAT'S OUR VIEW OF GOD?

Do we see Him as Creator? Almighty? Sovereign? In all the above verses, it says that God simply spoke and there it was. It seems humanly impossible to imagine the scope and height and depth of His creativity, enormity, and immensity! He simply spoke and there was the universe. It gives us breathless pause to consider the might and power of God and His awesomeness. All this is affirmed in 2 PET 3:5 when he writes, *"But they deliberately forget that long ago by God's word the heavens existed and the earth was formed out of water and by water."* NIV

I'm no expert but I understand that there is a galaxy out in the universe near us called Andromeda. In the galaxy Andromeda, there are four billion suns the same size as our one sun that warms our Earth. It is hard to imagine that there are four billion suns in Andromeda the same size as ours and we have only one. Yet the one sun that we do have is powerful enough to give us sunburn in the region of the Mason-Dixon Line of the U.S. in about twenty minutes if we're without protection. It's impossible to imagine the heat and light that's emitted in that area of the universe when there are four billion suns. The Bible says that God simply spoke and there they were. All that power in all forms of heat, light and radiation energy for eons and God simply spoke and there it was. It's enough to take one's breath away.

When I was a child, I thought there was only one type of banana. Now I've come to know that there are some fourteen varieties of bananas. There are bananas for eating, cooking, feeding pigs, baking, and whatever. God's creativity in all the varieties of earthly and marine life, plants and minerals that we have in our earth is incomprehensible. We only have to meditate on nature in all its variety and forms to come to the conclusion that there is none like God. He is all-powerful, creative, immense, and enormous.

Once while awaiting the arrival of a friend at the Singapore airport, I remember staring at a beautiful indigo blue colored fish in the huge aquarium in the waiting area. The fish seemed peculiar to me in that it had a very precise chartreuse colored band across its mid-section. In my gaze, I mused that the colors were somewhat mismatched, and I thought it made the fish look somewhat odd with the chartreuse contrasting so severely with that indigo blue. While idly engaged in my thoughts that it was a funny looking fish, a voice seemed to come up behind me, spoke right into my ear and said, "Oh yeah, let's see you make a fish!"

God is an awesome God. When one considers the variety of creation in vegetation, oceans, marine life, stars, moons, galaxies, heat, light, nuclear power, flowers, animals, our whole ecology, and even man, himself, it is difficult to stand under the weight of the knowledge of the immensity of God.

And there is something else....He is for us!....God is for us! All that enormity, all that immensity, all that power and creativity – God is for us. He's not against us. He's not disappointed in us. He's not angry with us. As we trust and obey, the all-knowing, all-wise, all-powerful God is for us. ***He wants to see us successful.*** He wants to see us fulfill all that He has in store for us and to achieve all that He has planned for us. God is for us! And if God be for us...what can be against us?

FOR FURTHER MEDITATION: PSM 90:1-2, PSM 115:3, PSM 135:5-7
ISAIAH 40:9-11, 55:11

WHAT'S OUR VIEW OF MAN? - HOW WE DO WE SEE OURSELVES?

John Steward of Australia shared some thoughts with this little scheme on what were meant to be the original, relational aspects of man to God and His Creation[6]

[6] John Steward, Brochure to The Gift That Releases (Australia: World Vision, 1994)

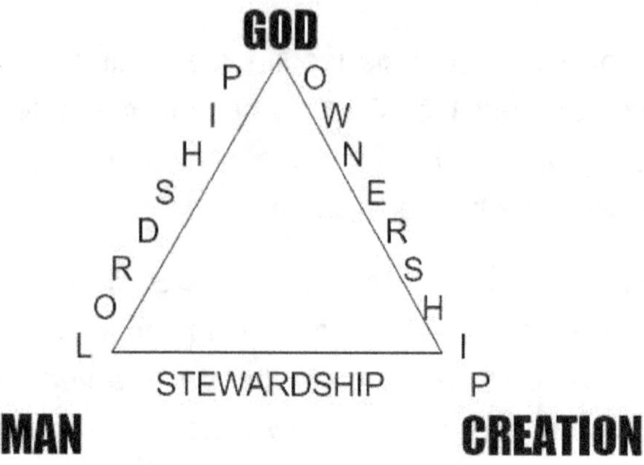

The original intention for man was that he would be in right relationship by recognizing the authority of God and submitting to Him as Lord. Further, that man would acknowledge God as the Owner of the universe by God's right of Creation, and that man would accept his responsibility as Steward of Creation in his obedience to the Lordship of God. As man followed the wisdom and dictates of God with this simple, social structure, there would be peace and harmony in the universe.

As we learn from Scripture and awful, historical, universal experience, man does not always desire to follow God's prescribed order but instead seeks to elevate himself by eliminating God from the picture. Secular forces around the globe, throughout history and even now, seek to remove the spiritual and religious guidance that God has established for man's successful living in harmony with Creation and other men.

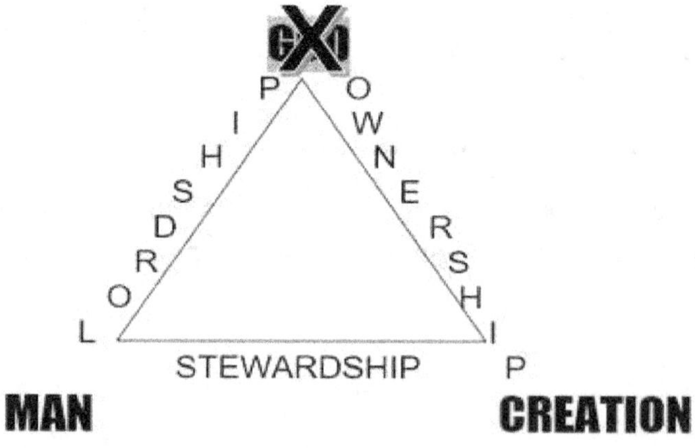

By eliminating God from this picture, man then considers himself the "lord" and "owner" of the universe, to the point that he believes he can do whatever he wants with it, even to the point of waste, destruction, and the enslavement of other men.

Man pays a heavy price for his rebellion against God since there has rarely been a period of real peace and harmony in the earth in the history of man.

DOES GOD HAVE A PLAN FOR THE DEVELOPMENT OF MAN?

LUKE 2:52 says that Jesus "grew" in wisdom, stature and in favor with God and men.[7]

JESUS "GREW"

MENTALLY / PHYSICALLY / SPIRITUALLY / SOCIALLY

There was increase to Jesus' development in all four components and since Jesus, in His uniqueness, is our model, we have a Godly pattern for the development of man.

This is affirmed similarly in MARK 12:30 that says we are to love God with our mind / strength / heart / soul.

We can infer that, if people are to grow to wholeness and be responsible, mature, human beings, these four components must have some semblance of being developed in their character formation and personalities. If growth is deficient or out of balance in any of these four areas, we will have people with hurtful character flaws, personality weaknesses, and behavioral struggles.

---

7 Bob Moffitt of Harvest Foundation, Phoenix, Arizona (www.harvestfoundation. org) is credited for his seminal thoughts on Lk 2:52 (YWAM School of Development lectures, Kona Hawaii, c.1988). Expanded use, exegesis, and commentary on Luke 2:52 are based on my own interpretation.

First, it says Jesus grew mentally. There was intellectual growth to Jesus. He must have been able to read the Scriptures as He was teaching in the temple when He was twelve years old. We are to love God with our minds. We function through our minds in making right, Godly choices. The highest decision we can make is simply to love God. Loving God is an act and decision of our mind by committing our will in obedience and loyalty to Him. It is peace with God.

ISAIAH 26:3 - "*Thou wilt keep him in perfect peace whose mind is set on Thee...*" KJV

On the other hand, man in rebellion, who believes he doesn't need God and leads his life independent of God, will eventually have the displeasure of God abiding on him. JOHN 3:36 - "*Whoever believes in the Son has eternal life, but whoever rejects the Son will not see life, for God's wrath remains on him.*" NIV

In development, if people are not given opportunity to grow mentally through some form of education, or training, whether informal or formal, the result most likely will be a person with social disabilities and doubts of their own adequacy, self-image, and esteem. It is common knowledge, that adults who are unable to read, write, or count go through life feeling inadequate but mostly fearful that someone will discover their disability. They silently suffer the risk of public exposure and will use various means to disguise their frailty. God's full intention toward us is that we should have the opportunity to grow mentally and that includes reading and writing. Decision-making, problem solving, and planning are all within the purview of mental development.

(Some sects put a strong emphasis on the mental component of development believing that through "mind expanding" and "meditation" techniques we will become a more "aware" person achieving new heights of power potential and sublimity. Adherents here do not realize that they could be opening themselves up to supernatural forces that could deceive and control their minds and eventually destroy them.)

Jesus grew physically. There was growth to Jesus' physical stature. Since Jesus lived to be a bright, young man, his living conditions were at least adequate to grow and develop to physical wholeness. He must have had an adequate food and water supply. Jesus had a job. He had an income to provide for his physical needs. Being a carpenter gave Him opportunity to pursue some creativity, be productive and avoid dependency.

One failure of the socio-liberal approach to solving societal problems is the emphasis on the economic aspects of people's needs. Our welfare systems, despite massive budgets expended to help people escape their poverty, create dependencies through their continual giving and counseling. They provide sad testimony in their failure to facilitate the development of our disadvantaged neighbors into whole, responsible, productive members of society. Failing to stimulate our less fortunate neighbors toward a more self-reliant approach keeps them mired in dependency.

Since the liberal assumption is that man is materialistic, they do not consider the spiritual elements of people that must be developed in matters of personal discipline, outlook, responsibility, attitude, accountability, and morality for true meaning, purpose, and vision for their lives. Man is not simply physical; he is spiritual and social as well.

Jesus grew spiritually. It is mystifying to learn that Jesus, in all His perfections, still had room to "grow," especially "in favor" with His heavenly Father Who already loved Him with an infinite love.

It is significant that Luke makes this declaration immediately after Jesus, at twelve years old, was found teaching in the temple by His parents who thought he was lost.

In his first recorded words, Jesus, in firmness with His parents, responds,

"...Did you not know I must be about my father's business?" LUKE 2:49 **NKJV-OB**

In what must have created a seismic event in the heavenlies, Jesus, at that moment, explicitly cast His bread upon the waters. This first, public expression of Jesus' commitment to embark on the Father's plan for His life, must have stirred the Father to great favor.

As the twelve-year-old grew physically, socially, in wisdom, and age, while moving incrementally, relentlessly, and flawlessly toward His ultimate purpose and destiny, it must have brought immeasurable, growing delight to the Father's heart.

Jesus grew socially. There was a social component to His development. Jesus grew in the esteem of men. Jesus was successful in His relationships. He was able to attract and harmonize a variety of discordant personalities into His personal, discipleship team.

Jesus had friends. He wept when Lazarus died. At Jericho He saw Zaccheaus up in a tree trying to get a better view of Jesus and his contingent. Jesus didn't insist that they meet in the synagogue to discuss Zaccheaus' spiritual condition. It was more like – *Zaccheaus, I'm coming over to your house for dinner.* (LUKE 19:2).

Jesus interacted and even socialized with some of his detractors and won the respect of His adversaries. Many, of course, were vehemently jealous of His successes which incited their disposition and plots against Him.

Nonetheless, Jesus models for us that to attain maturity and wholeness as persons, we need to grow and develop socially and be successful in our relationships.

If ever there was a time when we needed healers and peacemakers in relationships it is now. Runaway children, alienation within families, divorce rates skyrocketing, abuse of children, women and the unborn, increasing violence between nationalities, races, and religions, disrespect for law and law enforcement, unrestrained preoccupation with sexual liberties, immorality, drug and alcohol abuse, human trafficking are all manifestations of an accelerating breakdown in relationships. The world needs role models in how to live and promote successful relationships.

We should note that there was a special quality to Jesus' mental development. The mental component of His growth in **LUKE 2:52** is described as "wisdom." Jesus' "mental" development was undergirded by His "spiritual" growth, which was due to His intimate, relationship with the Father. Because of His submission in relationship to the Father, Jesus' mental development transcended the simple acquisition of knowledge and facts. He had attained "wisdom" which may be defined as *that unity of knowledge and understanding under the guidance of the Holy Spirit.* Wisdom is knowledge applied under the submission to the Holy Spirit.

The Bible tells us that in all our getting we ought to get wisdom because PROV 4:7 - *"Wisdom is supreme..."* **NIV**

ECCL 7:12 says wisdom is a lifesaver *"wisdom preserves the life of its possessor."* **NIV** Wisdom will be our rescue in times of crisis and our avoidance of trouble if we let it, but it is only available from God.

Apprehending this concept of "wisdom" is vital to the successful development of societies and a harmonious social order. Eliminating God from our deliberations inhibits our access to wisdom since God is the source of wisdom. PROV 2:6 - *" For the Lord gives wisdom..."* **NKJV-OB**

JAMES 1:5 - *"If any of you lacks wisdom, he should ask God who gives generously to all without finding fault, and it will be given to him.* **NIV**

We can readily observe that societies around the globe, are striving to eliminate all forms of religious presence, ceremony, and activity from public life. They consider religion a private matter that should not be practiced in open, public, or political forums.

The resultant tragedy of our day, evidenced by the continuing decline of nations and prevalence of hostilities, is that men and women of great intellectual capacity, holding positions of great power and influence, through indifference, presumption, and pride have minimized their own need for spiritual development and thereby forfeit their access to *wisdom*. We only need to survey the news to realize the world is in a dangerous, downward spiral economically and relationally. We're finding that the solutions of man have been inadequate or dismal failures. Man in submission was meant to have a vibrant and intimate relationship with God Who would grant him *wisdom* to face the world's challenges. By rejecting God and marginalizing His influence, man is thus compelled to rely on his own limited reasoning without the availability of *wisdom*.

JER 8:9 - *"The wise men will be put to shame; they will be dismayed and trapped, since they have rejected the word of the Lord; what kind of wisdom do they have?"* **NIV**

Without the wisdom of God, man must then use his own limited resources to face the challenges of life within the finite limits of his own faulty, imperfect knowledge.

SOME THOUGHTS ON "THE ABUNDANT LIFE"

Jesus says it is He Who came to give us life and give it to the full - JN 10:10. There is no conclusive definition of the Abundant Life in Scripture. The Fullness or "The Abundant Life," which only Jesus brings, is suggested to us again by **LUKE 2:52**.

Fullness of Life is not having our wants met but our needs met in the four areas of development: Mental / Physical / Spiritual / Social. It is not without contingencies.

There are conditions that must be existent for the Abundant Life to be attainable, otherwise, we shall experience deficits and the prospect of not having our needs met.

JOHN 8:36 - *"So if the son makes you free you will be free indeed."* **NIV**

2 COR 3:17 "*...where the Spirit of the Lord is there is freedom.*" **NIV**

Hence, conversely, where God is not welcome, there is no freedom.

In eliminating Christianity from our culture, as some are wont to do, forfeits the wisdom and providence of God while inviting diminished freedom. As societies become more hostile to a religious influence, attempt to marginalize spiritual activity and deny God, they shall incur the loss of freedoms. Where there is no freedom there is only bondage. Where there is bondage fullness of life is unattainable.

If Jesus is the embodiment of the only way, truth and life how can believers perceive life as being only spiritual in dimension without recognizing the physical and social needs of our fellow neighbors in society? Implicitly, the Lordship of Jesus ought to rule over all aspects of our social order. Yet, as Christians, we often act as if being participants and preoccupied with all aspects of church life is our only sacred duty.

How is it not our sacred duty to be active in the life and decision-making processes of our schools, government, media, arts, entertainment, and economy, if Jesus is the giver of abundant life? Not bringing the full-orbed abundant life to our communities is hardly the vision of loving our neighbor. Through our lack of care and participation, we leave the other areas of community and social concern to the dominance by secular forces.

Thus, whole nations are teetering on the brink of collapse and unable to resolve their difficulties because of their refusal to acknowledge that God is the source of all benefits. Indifference or denial of His presence forfeits access to His wisdom and, at the same time, brings the lack of fullness of life and developmental deficits upon themselves. In pride and rebellion, what peace they forfeit. LUKE 23:34 - *"...Father, forgive them for they know not what they do."* NKJV-OB

****

ACTS 6:1-6 - reminds us that we need to keep the four components for growth in a kind of balance. It is possible to be "so spiritually minded we become no earthly good." Christians can be knowledgeable about spiritual matters yet unaffected by the social or physical needs of people around them. The leaders, in this passage, corrected their oversight.

It is interesting, however, according to this passage that most matters, in the final analysis, tend to be spiritual in nature. Our misguided, secularized world would have us believe that all matters are political or at least dialyzed between political and spiritual, with the emphasis on political. Here, the Grecian Christians were to select *spirit-filled men of high character and wisdom* for something as mundane and earthly as *waiting on tables.* In God' s intentions for this world, all matters in Creation touch the spiritual.

Still,we're cautioned against communicating a Christianity that's legal or unresponsive and not one that's loving, sensitive, compassionate, and relational.

A DEVELOPMENT MODEL FOR COMMUNITIES

As **LUKE 2:52** speaks of Jesus' growth in mental/physical/spiritual/social components that gives us a model for man, we can enlarge its use as a model for the development of communities.

Following the Jesus model, communities can be envisioned to develop similarly in the four areas of development. Using **LUKE 2:52** can help us observe and assess deficits in all aspects of community life like schools, food production, health care, employment, even spiritual and social life. Where deficits occur in any of these components, we have starting points for change.

The following, simple chart can facilitate our evaluations of community life. We can add other probing topics to our chart at will. Developing the chart into something more sophisticated can serve as a real tool in evaluating a community's potential. Journaling our findings will help us build a database for the use of others as well.

LUKE 2:52

MENTAL	*PHYSICAL*	*SPIRITUAL*	*SOCIAL*
LITERACY % ?	WATER ?	FREEDOM ?	CONFLICT/RACE?
EDUCATION OPPS?	FOOD SOURCES?	CHURCHES?	VICES/GAMBLING?
FACILITIES?	WORK AVAILABLE?	DISCIPLING?	FAMILY LIFE?
TEACHERS ?	HOUSING ?	GROWING?	LAWS ENFORCED?
LEVELS ?	HEALTH/CLINICS ?	"GOING?"	CRIME RATES?
SCHOOLS?	ENERGY ?	OCCULT?	DRUGS/AIDS ?

****

This article from the Solomon Islands involved a local complaint on an educational tool used to survey the people's views on development as they experienced it. Again, we apologize for the low quality of the reprint.

It addresses three areas of concern in village life development. We show it here only to contrast it with our view that there are four areas of development, the fourth being the spiritual element as revealed by **LUKE 2:52**. We can only speculate why the spiritual element in the Wheel article was omitted.

DEVELOPMENT WHEEL

A COMPLAINT

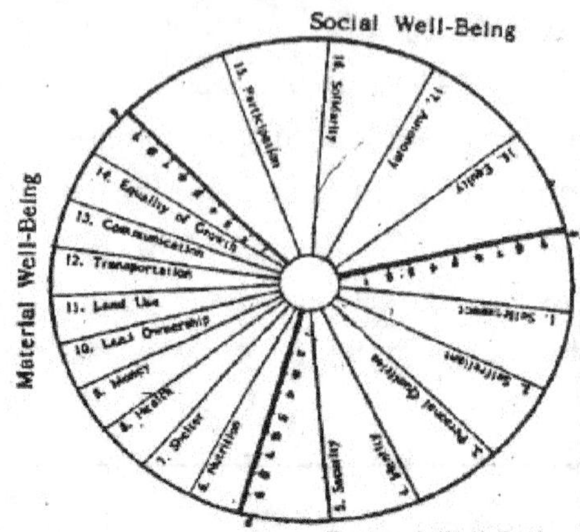

During a development education workshop at Savo one of the villagers, David Sade, had some reservations concerning the meaning of SIDT's education tool, the Development Wheel.

He argued that the Development Wheel is being used to discourage or stop villagers from doing business or participating in rural area development projects.

Below is a brief explanation of the purpose of the development wheel.

The Development Wheel is one of the development education tools that SIDT mobile teams use in the rural areas when they discuss development and the well-being of the people.

It helps villagers analyse the different areas of their life and see if development is taking place in those areas or not.

If there is a low score in one area, then development of a country, or a village, or a person is not balanced. SIDT believes there are three areas of development. These are the development of the person, the society in which the person belongs and the development of the material things the person needs.

In the Development Wheel picture picture, these three areas are called Personal Well-being, Social Well-being and Material Well-being.

When people are given a copy of the Development Wheel to score about their own life situations, it is an exercise that is often done during a development education workshop to see how people assess their own lives as they are today.

So the Development Wheel is not an instrument used to stop villagers running businesses or to discourage them from making money from their own projects. The Wheel is simply used to help people see the meaning of having a high score in one area of life while scoring low in another.

In other words it makes the participants think about what part of their life situation needs to be changed so that they work hard to develop it.

DOES GOD HAVE A PLAN FOR MAN TO BE A DEVELOPER?

THE DOMINION MANDATE GEN 1:28

"BE FRUITFUL" - BE PRODUCTIVE

MULTIPLY – INCREASE "

FILL" - MALA - FULFILL

- RESOURCE DEVELOPMENT

- EXPLORATION – JOB 28:

- INVENTION / RESEARCH

SUBDUE - HARNESS

- NOT BE SUBJECT TO

DOMINION – CONTROL – MANAGE – STEWARDSHIP

GEN 1:28 - This Scripture is often referred to as the Dominion Mandate. God has commissioned us to exercise dominion in the earth. He calls on man to be a *co-creator* with Himself.

In my early days as a newly converted Christian, I was puzzled over the translations of these verses which always suggested they involved the command to have a lot of children. Be fruitful – have a lot of children! Multiply and have a lot of children! Fill the earth and have a lot of children. I was mystified as to why the Lord would repeat Himself three times in just one verse. Later I realized, with some word study, that there were different possibilities for these translations that could suggest something more in the way of development rather than just procreation.

TO BE FRUITFUL - could likely be translated "to be industrious" or "productive." God has given us the brains and muscle to do work that we might be producers. As humans, we were being commissioned to exert effort to benefit from the "fruit" of our labors.

MULTIPLY - might well be translated "increase" - that God wants us to take what He has given us and increase it. If we grow melons of a certain size, we ought to produce larger ones. If we can produce one ear of corn, God would have us increase it to two.

FILL - This word could have the connotation to "fulfill" the earth (not only necessarily to fill it with children). In God's creation, the earth too has a destiny. It yearns as we do for redemption - ROM 8:21-22. We are to bring and employ the earth to its full potential. God wants us to be creative with invention, exploration, and discovery. JOB 28 speaks of mining, and precious metals and jewels hidden in the earth. God wants us to explore and discover oil, gas, nuclear, and solar power as resources for our comfort and convenience. We can be inventive and desalinate oceans for our water needs. Learning skills for composting, proper fertilizing of soil, irrigation and techniques to prevent soil erosion can increase our harvests and food production. With faith, our prospects can be limitless if we step up with confidence and be industrious to discover what the Lord has for us on land and in the sea.

<u>SUBDUE</u> - Some past translations have been hurtful toward our understanding of what God would have us do with the earth. The notion of "subdue" has a negative connotation suggesting that we are to quash the earth and or do with it whatever we please. In our limited English, this word could have been better translated as "harness."

We are to harness and capture nature's resources, convert and employ them for the benefit of mankind. Recently, there are great advances being made in renewable energy sources such as solar, geo-thermal, hydroelectric, and wind systems producing large of amounts of electrical power. God wants us to harness resources to make them more available for blessing mankind.

Once, on visiting a friend in India on the western border near Pakistan, he chose to accommodate me with a room in a nice hotel near his neighborhood. It was a favorite stop for traveling salesmen through that area and I was surprised by the quality of the hotel in such a remote part of India. Further, I was astonished by the fact that they had hot running water in the sinks and showers twenty-four hours a day. They had a constant supply of hot water for their laundry, cooking, and washing needs all day long. That was very unusual for India in those days, especially in such a remote part of the country. While on a walk a short distance from the hotel, I looked back and saw that the roof of the hotel was completely covered with solar panels. They were using solar panels to harness the heat from the sun to produce heating for their water needs twenty-four hours a day. The Lord says we can "harness" nature and its power for our benefit by being industrious and bringing the earth and its resources up to their full potential.

<u>DOMINION</u> - God intended that man be a co-creator with Him by telling us to increase and multiply what there is. Included in the Dominion Mandate, expressed by two Hebrew words SHARMA and ABAD, is the notion that in all our doing we are to be mindful that it is for the management and care of someone else – God.

We are the beneficiaries of our endeavors, yet we are to exercise diligence, since all that is intended to benefit us is only consigned to us. Being protective of resources and conserving what God has given us are part of His plan. In the enjoyment of the advances, comforts, and conveniences of our efforts, we are to be good managers in all that we undertake. The term best used is stewardship. We are to be good stewards.

"ABAD" - TO TILL, AS A SERVANT
UNTO A MASTER
"SHARMA"- TO GUARD, TO BE DILIGENT OVER FOR ANOTHER, AS IN STEWARDSHIP

Loving our neighbor through stewardship requires the righteous use of resources. God's intention is for man to use all that has been consigned to him but that our provision is not to be squandered or wasted. Loving our neighbor requires that we be mindful of the future generations that follow. Often lacking in our understanding, however, is that good stewardship involves increasing our resources as well as managing them. Managing all there is commendable but in the parable of the talents, God praises the entrepreneurial spirit. We need to get beyond the constriction that good stewarding is basically preserving, rationing or hoarding God's provision. Certainly, believers ought to be role models of conservation. But we do need to get beyond the mind-set that rationing or hoarding our resources is necessary because that's all there is - or that exploration, discovery, or mining of new resources are somehow destructive to God's overall plan. We honor and respect the beauty and glories of nature but not worship them, and at the same time, we are to be co-creators with God.

The task for man is to obey the command to exercise *dominion*. God's challenge to man is to pursue the development of creation to its full potential, not only of man but of nature as well.

It's interesting to note that the Bible begins with Genesis in the garden and ends with Revelation in a city. God in His foresight understood that man through his obedience to the dominion mandate, having begun in an agrarian lifestyle, through curiosities, explorations, inventions, and discoveries would eventually produce something as complex as a city – with super highways, automobiles, television, cat scans, microwaves, artificial kidneys, airports, ships, rockets, cell phones, computers, lasers, pacemakers, and all the interminable gadgets and inventions that make our life comfortable, safe, and convenient. There seems to be no limit as to what man might achieve through the industrious use of his talents.

It all began with development. Development began when people recognized and focused on a problem, a need, or desire for improvement. Man was challenged with the task of dominion. What was required was the strategy to solve the problem, with a vision of how the outcome should look. Assessing a community's need and defining the basic strategy to achieve the objective becomes a key in the approach to improving its outcome.

If we were to state "dominion" as the community development goal we might use this following, simple chart. Our chart here illustrates a crude, fundamental plan that states the problem, states a simple strategy toward solving the problem , and illustrates what skills a community developer might use in facilitating its resolution. Finally, what ought to be the response of the people for accomplishing the goal.

Crude as it is, this chart can be used as a handy tool to teach people a basic planning skill. It is a simple key to encourage a clear, focused statement of the problem to enhance the process in pursuing basic community development.

So in our little planning schematic we insert "dominion" as our problem. God' s strategy for the development of man to exercise dominion is work (industry, effort). Work is God's sacred strategy for man not only to exercise dominion but for man to grow and develop to his full potential.

GEN 2:15 - "*Then the Lord God took the man and put him in the Garden of Eden to tend it and keep it.*" **NKJV-OB**

PROBLEM	-	dominion
STRATEGY	-	work

In the garden, Adam had all his needs met. He had a relationship with God and 100% Quality of Life, yet God gave him work to do. He was to till the garden and look after it. Despite the fact that Adam could luxuriate in all God had given him according to GEN 2:15, God in His wisdom gave Adam the strategy to exercise dominion - work. Work was instituted before the fall of man and thus must be looked on as "sacred." It is an important principle for people in development to understand the value of work.

In some cultures, work is looked on as a curse or for women and children, or slaves. Work is not a curse; it is God's sacred strategy for the development of man to exercise dominion.

God gives us the freedom to choose and pursue work according to our calling, giftings, and preferences that we might grow into wholeness mentally, physically, spiritually, and socially. We each have a part to play in exercising dominion. One might be a nurse, policeman, lawyer, farmer, mechanic, poet, musician, or teacher and fulfill one's part in exercising dominion within that sphere of endeavor. The choice remains up to us. Our challenge is to use our God-given creative abilities and faculties to whatever goals and limits we want to exert them. We can be lazy, choose not to pursue any options God has given us and actually thwart our own development. We can hinder God's intentions for us by being slack, fatalistically believing the system discriminates against us, claiming entitlements, expecting others to do it for us, or believing that we're inadequate to the task.

Certainly, there are times when crises arise wherein people need outside help through stressful periods. Sudden job loss or disability can prevent us from exercising the freedom to pursue our desires and fulfill our call to dominion. There are systems that are full of injustice that present barriers to development. Dishonest landlords, dishonest politicians, high crime rates, civil strife can all hinder development. But we ought to recognize also that there are social policies and programs that lessen man's call to work and thus inhibit his creative abilities to productivity and dominion. Programs of this sort, well intentioned though they may be, hinder man's mandated strategy to grow and develop to his full potential. When crises strike and relief is the needed intervention, we must keep in mind the need to help but attempt to move recipients out of the Relief mode into a development mode as quickly as possible. We want to avoid the snare of dependency and ensure their continuing growth and development into the abundance of life. This holds true for individuals, communities, and even nations.

LUKE 2:52 alerts us to the fact that there are four dimensions to man's development and not just the physical and economic ones. The worldview that claims man to be purely an economic and physical animal is contradicted by biblical truth. That man shall not live by bread alone but by every word of God has been overwhelmingly confirmed by life experience. The spiritual and social aspects of man's development take on an exhilarating tone when he is allowed to be creative and imaginative in pursuing outcomes of his own aspirations. It can have satisfying results. God's strategy for our growth is for mankind to progress to wholeness through his exertion, industry, and work.

God as the community development change agent *enabled* man to get the job done. God equipped man with strength, muscles, and a brain to identify and solve problems. God's skill in facilitating man was that of an enabler. Man's necessary response to God's initiatives is to step up to responsibility and work.

Through this simple chart, we can make a theological statement, not necessarily for its profundity but for its ease and usefulness. If we needed to justify the ministry of community development to theologians who might feel that it is not a legitimate biblically based ministry, we could use this little chart to explore its validity.

PROBLEM - DOMINION
STRATEGY - WORK
SKILL OF C.D WORKER (GOD) - ENABLER
RESPONSE OF MAN - RESPONSIBILITY

Man's task is dominion which is accomplished through the strategy of work for which he has been enabled. Man's necessary response is to step up to responsibility and work as unto the Lord and not half-hardheartedly or remissly.

■ September 1995

OUR DAILY BREAD®

For Personal and Family Devotions

September 4
Monday

GOD-HONORING WORK

READ:
Proverbs 27:23-27

Let him labor, working with his hands what is good.
—Ephesians 4:28

Several years ago in the South African territory of Kwa-Zulu, the government dug irrigation ditches on both sides of a river. This allowed the rich land to be farmed. The Christian Zulus on one side of the river produced lush crops and prospered. The traditional animist worshipers on the other side continued to live in abject poverty, producing almost nothing on the same kind of soil.

Why? The Christians believed they were responsible before God to work hard and live soberly. Their pagan neighbors, on the other hand, viewed work as the women's responsibility, while the men spent their time drinking and fighting.

THE BIBLE IN ONE YEAR:
☐ Ezekiel 1–3

The Bible tells us that as God's image-bearers we are to "have dominion over . . . every living thing that moves on the earth" (Gen. 1:28). It urges us to work with our hands so that we can provide for ourselves and others (Eph. 4:28; 1 Th. 4:11). Work, when performed with the right attitude, can be pleasurable and rewarding. Proverbs 27:23-27 portrays the beautiful interplay of diligent work on our part and faithful nurture on God's.

Whatever your job, do it diligently and gratefully. Through it you will find pleasure and experience God's blessing. —HVL

We thank You, Lord, for giving us
The opportunity
To work to earn our daily bread
And share it willingly. —Sper

WHEN GOD PUTS WORK INTO YOUR LIFE, HE EXPECTS YOU TO PUT LIFE INTO YOUR WORK.

WRITERS:
Henry G. Bosch • J. David Branon • Dennis J. De Haan
Martin R. De Haan II • Richard W. De Haan
David C. Egner • Vernon C. Grounds • Haddon W. Robinson
Herbert Vander Lugt • Joanie E. Yoder

ACKNOWLEDGMENTS:
Cover Photo: Ron Thomas / FPG International
Scripture quotations are from the New King James Version,

MANAGING EDITOR: Kurt De Haan • EDITOR: Dennis De Haan
SENIOR EDITOR: Mr. Clair Hess • ASSISTANT EDITOR: Tim Gustafson
STAFF EDITORS: David Sper, Anne Bierema • EDITORIAL ASSISTANT: Lisa Wadin

 Volume 40, Number 6 • Printed in USA

WHAT'S OUR VIEW OF MAN? HOW DO WE SEE OURSELVES?

WHAT'S MAN'S POTENTIAL? HOW FAR CAN HE GO?

In Genesis 11, God's own testimony declares (although not in a very edifying way) that man has the potential to achieve anything he decides to do. Even while bringing indictment, God suggests there is no limit to man's potential. At the same time, we see God's disdain for man's abuse of his skills and talents in perverting them toward idolatrous and self-serving pursuits. God was not pleased with the perversion of His intentions for man, so as a consequence, in His wisdom, disrupted all the plans of man and thwarted his self-indulgent tendencies.

We do live in the Age of Babel re-visited as man seeks in so many ways to achieve reckless and irresponsible innovations that remind us again that man is not always wise and scrupulous in his undertakings. The Babel experience suggests there is something within man that would push us beyond rational boundaries to any and all extremes regardless of the implications. Man's pursuit of recognition, fame, and prizes motivates him toward endeavors that often strike aversion in the hearts of ordinary laymen.

Medical journals across the globe report on growing research fraud involving " altering or fabricating data" in various undertakings mostly in order to win grants and awards. It appears in many quarters Science would have no accountability to God or man. Under a relativistic worldview, it is often indifferent to morality or ethics in its pursuits – with no safeguards, no ethical parameters, still denying the supernatural or non- rational, and insisting on being self- regulated. Our societal, secular drift could allow Science to become anarchical.

We have so much to be grateful for to our scientific community. With all the incredible advances medically and technologically, life in the twenty - first century has been served by a countless number of innovations and scientific developments to endow us with unimagined health, comforts, conveniences and unparalleled enjoyment. But until Science generates something of a *philosophy of science* to foster some modicum of peer review or restraint on the types of research that intimidate our sensibilities and values, many of us will be restless and un-approving of many of science's endeavors.

STUDY AND MEDITATE ON PSALM 8

CHAPTER EIGHT: *IT'S NOT EASY BUT IT CAN BE DONE!*

HINDRANCES TO DEVELOPMENT

We ought to recognize that development work is not always easy. There are serious barriers, not always discernable, that can hinder progress. We ought to examine some of those now.

1) SIN - A major hindrance to development is the selfishness and rebellion in the hearts of men. The reason there is poverty in the earth is because of sin. Poverty in the earth is not God's intention. His original intention was for us to be happy and content in our relationship with Him.

When Adam was created, he had everything he wanted. He had a direct relationship with God, and all his needs met. He had a 100% Quality of Life. When he sinned, he became impoverished and death, degeneration, and poverty were introduced in the earth. We need to understand this clearly because in some cultures it is maintained that it is God's will that people be poor.

If one believes it's God's will that people be poor then any effort to escape their poverty would be acting contrary to the will of God. Hence, peoples remain mired in poverty and underdevelopment because of their belief system which is rooted in a fatalistic worldview. God does not want people to be poor. It is the negative, evil, selfish, and spiritual forces that want to keep people under – to keep them in ignorance, in ill health, and in social chaos and strife.

Is it possible to believe that our loving God and Father of Whom the Scriptures say owns the cattle on a thousand hills (PSM 50:10) and the earth and all its fullness (PSM 24:1) would hoard all that for Himself?

ROM 8:3 says that God gave us the ultimate in Jesus. He who gave us His only begotten Son, would He not give us all other things besides? Since He's already given us the ultimate, why would He hold anything back when all other things are lesser?

****

There is success and blessing in obedience to His ways. Obedience as one of the keys to prosperity is found in 2 CHR 24:20. So if sin and selfishness are a problem in development, then God's ways will have to be brought into it. Rebellion, greed, covetousness can enter in and whatever progress has been made could be temporary. The development process can weaken and disintegrate. To reinforce our efforts, biblical principles need to be integrated into the development process. People have got to be brought into God's way of doing things so that they might receive the blessings that come with obedience. Otherwise, improvement won't last.

There will be circumstances when we may not yet be able to bring God into it because of the spiritual climate in which we work, especially in a location that is adversarial to Christianity. Instilling God's principles must be on our agenda, however.

We can establish kingdom of God principles, even with non-believers, without ever mentioning the name of the Lord. Principles of giving, sharing, forgiving, being like-minded in community spirit can be encouraged to counteract selfishness for the work to endure. Vices like gambling, fighting, drunkenness, and spousal abuse, which are detrimental to community life, must be resisted and spoken against. Ethical and spiritual content must be brought into the development process, even without proselytizing, or else it will be vulnerable to rivalries, jealousies, and selfishness.

A natural, restrainer to selfishness in a community is a church. Ultimately, Church planting must be on our agenda to establish a buffer of resistance to sin and selfishness. An active church will be a permanent restrainer to establish stability and harmony in the community. Otherwise, our work will be temporary.

But what is a church? How do we know we have a church? What will the church be doing? A church is not a building, it is simply a gathering (MATT 18:20) – a gathering where people are obeying the seven commands of Jesus.

The commands of Jesus are as we've discussed them before:

1) Repenting and believing
2) Being baptized
3) Loving God, neighbor, enemy
4) Celebrating the Lord's Supper
5) Praying
6) Giving – tithing, stewardship, righteous use of money
7) Going – witnessing – making disciples, preaching

At a Seoul train station during our Olympic outreach there was an elderly gentleman who patiently listened to our gospel message. When he seemed responsive enough, I asked if he wanted to become a Christian. Although he was interested, he said there was no point in becoming a Christian because he would never be able to attend church. He was at the train station to go back home. Where he lived was in such a remote area that it was about 100 miles from the nearest church. His reasoning was that since he could not attend church there was no point in becoming a Christian. I showed him that a church was simply a gathering of two or three Christians and that a plan for him would be first, to become a Christian, and go back to his home area and make two or three other Christians. When he understood that he could start a church right there where he lived, he became gleeful at that news. He bowed his head, prayed with us to become a Christian, and ran off exuberantly to his train.

(On the righteous use of money, Peter Batchelor relates the story of the farmers in Papua New Guinea who received 40 million dollars from the U.S. on a contract for their coffee. It is estimated that 20 million dollars of that income went toward the purchase of alcoholic beverages.)[8]

The righteous use of money is not only good stewardship it is a principle of development.

2) THE COMMUNITY DEVELOPMENT WORKERS THEMSELVES - C.D. workers can be a hindrance and their own worst enemy. It's especially true in cross-cultural situations or in environments generally unfamiliar to their normal lifestyle.

An unwillingness to adjust to the habits, behavior, and customs of the ministry location can ruin one's effectiveness as a change agent. We need to be adaptable.

Every one of us has a measure of *ethno-centricity* which, unknowingly or not, would have us believe that our own culture is a more superior to all others. It is a common human trait to believe that one's culture is more acceptable with its foundations of values and traditions. Holding to this belief in a strange culture can be offensive if one desires to avoid appearing paternalistic. A continuing lack of acculturation will hinder acceptance and trust of the worker who will be seen as an outsider by the community.

Poor attitudes of the worker are detrimental to the need of developing working and partnering relationships with the community. The three hurtful Cs of Complaining, Criticizing, and Condemning will convey an attitude of arrogance, haughtiness, and superiority that, in the extreme, will incite rejection of the worker by the community. Most of us have little patience with a whiner.

8 Peter Batchelor- People In Rural Development (Exeter, U.K.: The Paternoster Press, 1984) p 36

Insensitivity to relationships will also impede harmony with the community. Uncaring approaches and tactless interactions especially with leaders and those in authority can cause rifts that may go beyond repair. Developing skills as a "people person" is virtually mandatory if one really hopes to be successful in bringing beneficial change. Insensitivity to the customs of the community can cause serious barriers to success.

Unbelief of the worker is a great hindrance to development. We can expect results too quickly. Believing that God isn't with us or that He can't do it will destroy a worker's confidence and positive approaches to the work.

We need to believe that God is big enough for whatever challenges we face. *(That's why we went through our previous discussion on the awesomeness and immensity of God. God is for us.).* Don't be tempted to backslide into unbelief. God is bigger than anything we can face and wants to see us successful.

3) SPIRIT FORCES - People under a "spirit" of oppression will be filled with fears while tenaciously holding to superstitions, folk-gossip or traditions. It can infest entire communities.

One of my Cambodian refugee workers did not want to go to the hospital in the refugee camp. Secretly he continued to work with a boil the size of a golf ball on the back of his thigh. It was painful and caused him to favor his walk with a limp. Refugees were paid a small stipend for their work so he didn't want to miss out on the income. Further, he was afraid of going to the hospital for treatment because of the past history and experience in his home country under the despotic Pol Pot regime. He was actually fearful that he would be used for strange, experimental purposes in the hospital.

When I discovered his secret and finally insisted and personally took him to the sick bay room of the camp hospital run by Catholic Relief Services, he was able to receive the necessary treatment and in a few days, his boil was well on the way to healing.

Superstition, fear, tradition, isolation, inferiority, low self-esteem, worthlessness in the hearts and minds of people can all be hindrances to development. It will keep people under with little expectation or motivation to change.

4) "CULTURE OF POVERTY" - as defined by Oscar Lewis is "a poverty way of perceiving and integrating reality, as opposed to poverty as being an economic condition."[9]

This can be a huge barrier to development when this sentiment is widespread in a community. In this mind set, due to lack of any positive life experience, people will simply accept and accommodate their poverty as being an expected outcome. They might have the rationale that suggests, my father was poor, my grandfather was poor, and I'm poor, so what's new? They accept their poverty as being an inevitable condition so make little effort to change.

5) ETHIC OF UNDERDEVELOPMENT - Development often hinges on what people believe about the way things are. This can lead to lethargy that is often accompanied by blame shifting for a people's poverty condition. "We're poor because the rich are rich." "We're poor because God hasn't blessed us." "We're poor because of colonialism (or slavery)." We need to avoid clichés that make prejudiced, erratic assumptions that people are poor because they are somehow victims.

Situations obviously exist where there is gross injustice and oppression and where greed and selfishness exist to such a degree that the rich do get rich at the expense of the poor. If compounded with low education or poor family stability their situation becomes somewhat dire. Those situations are not universal, however, and failure oftentimes to admit the poor are poor simply because of inertia and apathy can cause lingering harm to their condition. Many times misplaced compassion and insensible excuses weigh against exposing hurtful attitudes in the hearts and minds of the people that corrodes their aspirations and keeps them underdeveloped.

The reasons for underdevelopment are quite often "spiritual." Absence of inner strength, low self-worth, feelings of inferiority, feelings of inadequacy, lack of hope and vision, all can lead to apathy and resignation. What is needed by individuals and communities that languish in underdevelopment is an internal critique.

Darrow Miller's excellent analysis in *The Development Ethic* of this condition suggests a worldview that is poor in spirit. "The hearts and minds of its people

---

9 David Stravers, Worldview, Religious Conversion and Poverty, (Pasadena, CA: Fuller Theological Seminary1983) p.5-6

play a larger role in a nation's development than its circumstances or natural resources. Different life perspectives yield different levels of development."[10]

Blame shifting becomes a default position of people who refuse to undergo an "internal critique" as indicated by Miller. They simply refuse to examine the possibility that their poverty condition and inertia may be a result of faults within themselves due to critical, negative attitudes. They see their problems as being caused by external factors and so expect solutions to their problems to come from the outside. They may expect and demand paternalism. They can be indifferent to the snares of dependency.

Without an honest appraisal of the reasons for their poverty and acceptance of responsibility and accountability for their condition, they can remain largely poor. *"The belief and attitude in the hearts and minds of the people who do not exercise an inner critique can be the most singular reason for the lack of development in their communities."*[11]

6) FATALISM - This is a crippling mind-set that leads to inertia because of resignation or a fatal disbelief that anything can change. It may be rooted in hopelessness. It can occur as religious belief that a poverty condition is a result of God's will. Since it is God's will, any attempt to change their poverty condition would be working against Him. Hence, they remain largely poor with no motivation to change. They feel all attempts will inevitably fail because of God's predetermined fate for them to be poor.

These three aforementioned mind-sets of the *Culture of Poverty, Ethic of Under-Development, and Fatalism* can be prevalent and dynamically operating in communities all at the same time. They are rooted in a faulty understanding of the character of God. It is difficult to overcome this complex of worldview deficiencies without a strong, spiritual approach that brings knowledge and revelation of the true nature of God. They need to know something of God's true character and loving intentions for their lives

"I began to pray for the sick and show them that it was God's will for them to have three meals a day, to be clothed properly, and live in a sanitary place. And I stressed it was God's will that they should rise and believe. By and by, our people began to be encouraged. They began to smile. They began to believe and find jobs; they began to create the job; that was amazing. They were so encouraged they began to create many jobs, from brick making to garbage gathering. They began to create the work.

---

10 Darrow Miller, The Development Ethic, (Scottsdale Arizona: Food for the Hungry 1988) p. 1

11 Darrow Miller, The Development Ethic, p 2-3

I tell you I'm just proud of them today because out of that utterly poverty-stricken place, they gave enough money to buy land and build a beautiful sanctuary.

And now when I go there, it is one of the richest residential areas. I can't find any slums left because the people all began to work and to have three meals a day."

Pastor Yonggi Cho 1985, 6 th Church Growth Conference

MEDITATE ON CHARACTER OF GOD

ISAIAH CHAPTERS 40-44, 50

7) CONFORMIST THINKING – Peer pressure, community and culture imposed uniformity can discourage individual initiative and greatly limit development improvements. Those forces can squelch independent voices from speaking boldly for change. Jealousy, competitiveness, rivalries can thwart possibilities for development efforts. Criticism or condescension, directed at innovators bringing improvements, can discourage their determination when having to face unreasonable, stubborn opposition.

In Australia there is something known as the Tall Poppy Syndrome. The sentiment is akin to something like this; in a field of poppies, if one poppy outgrows the others and becomes taller than the rest, the other poppies will seek to cut the tall poppy down.

Instead of trying to imitate the tall poppy and learn how it managed to grow so tall, in their jealousy and resentment the other poppies will seek to cut the tall poppy down to make it conform like the rest.

So it goes with people in communities that surpass the performance of others. They can often be victimized by pressures opposing them to conform like the rest

.

It can be said for the American culture, without boast, that generally when someone succeeds they are applauded and publicized and their efforts imitated with hopes that their success might be replicated. Books about them become best sellers as others hope to achieve the same success. Complaints about legitimate achievement don't seem to be that common in America. Still, conformist thinking otherwise can greatly inhibit development

8) REACTIVE FORCES - There can be active opposing forces that seek to limit efforts to bring development. These are so-called "reactive" to denote external, hindering forces that will work against those trying to bring change to help the poor. Injustices operating at the hands of dishonest landlords, corrupt officials, dishonest politicians, high crime, drug wars, unstable governments, and violence are huge hindrances to development activities. Community development relies on stable, harmonious, community cooperation and unity. Development is virtually impossible in unstable environments where risk is great to the security of the people and development workers.

Then too, communities that carry the mind-set of expecting paternalism without regard to the snares of dependency can also be reactive against true development efforts. They can have the expectancy of outside solutions to their problems which is detrimental to people's growth and development.

In Third World situations, the expectations of needy relatives to share in the fruits of those who achieve returns on their hard work can discourage their future efforts. Innovators who are put upon by demanding, less industrious extended family often suffer discouragement to the point of abandoning their own desire for improvement.

9) SELF-SEEKERS - Sociological studies inform us that, as a rudimentary principle, there are basically four personality types that can be found in any sizable group of people.[12]

One can test this theory simply by observing the several personality types that one encounters in any congregate of people. It is easily discernable among the residents in a neighborly community setting. For our purposes, we sort them with descriptions of more commonly observable behavior patterns in community

. A) The ***Self-Seekers*** are distinguishable by their highly motivated personalities. They can be usually found in the vicinity of leader activity. They easily circulate among those in authority or power. They will usually seek out the leaders to make suggestions or make complaints and be adept at acquiring information and latest news. They can be high-risk takers and are usually in the forefront of any community activity.

The problem with this type is that they are usually not community-minded. They are usually driven by self-interest and wait for no one. You rarely need to

[12] Dr. D. W. Ekstrand, The Four Human Temperaments (Tempe, Arizona: The Transformed Soul, 2012). We use Dr. Ekstrand's instructive article here only as one sample of the many published analyses of these types of personalities.

seek them out, they will usually come to you. It's not helpful to edify just these few individuals. Too much attention given to the self-seekers can be detrimental. For a change agent to align one's self with this personality type will be frowned upon by the other citizens and can cost the change agent the support of the more community-minded individuals. Our goal ought to be to benefit as many people as possible and not just an elite few. In religious parlance, these self-seekers might even be the first ones to seek conversion to be in the forefront and interact with those they perceive to be in authority. Happily, this type of personality will make up only a small percentage of the entire group, usually anywhere from 8 -10% of the population.

B) The ***Implementers*** make up the next category of personalities. This group is highly motivated but not to the extent as the Self-Seekers. This is the stable core of any group and generally represents the solid citizens of any community.

They are open to change for the better, would like a secure community, good schools, stable civic life, prosperity and harmony and would be willing to work for it. They are community minded and can often speak with wisdom, concern, and authority.

They can be open to risks but would need to be approached with respect and congeniality. These solid folks make up a major portion of the population of any community at about 40% and are the group with which the community development worker should identify and work. This group must be in the forefront in bringing change. They can take some risks. You go to them. Without their participation and influence, change will be difficult or short-lived.

C) The ***Followers***. This category of persons might not be as motivated as the other groups but they are "***motivatable.***" Given the right circumstances and safeguards, they are persuadable to make choices and take action. They are approachable with suggestions of change but may need to be convinced, reassured, and coached. They are also civic minded, solid citizens, desire wholesome community life and are willing to work at it. As a group, they might be more inclined to "wait and see" and join in the action after witnessing what others might be doing and thinking as initiators. Like the implementers, they are concerned and dependable. They too, make up a large portion of the population to the average of about 40%. Their participation is essential as well. These might need assurances and coaching.

D) The ***Resisters*** make up the last group and they are the most difficult with which to work. They simply reject you. Often mistrusting or feeling hopeless, they simply resign themselves to isolation and working alone or only with others of similar levels of apathy. Previous disappointments can cloud their aspirations, thus they may not participate to avoid further hurts or failures. Often they may feel without options or a voice of any kind.

Trying to work with this type can drain a worker's energies, stamina, and patience. They may require continual counseling or persuasion that often seems fruitless. One's energies might be better spent elsewhere. This group, however, only makes up a small portion of any community to the tune of about 10%.

In a simplified graphic this distribution of personalities would look something like this:

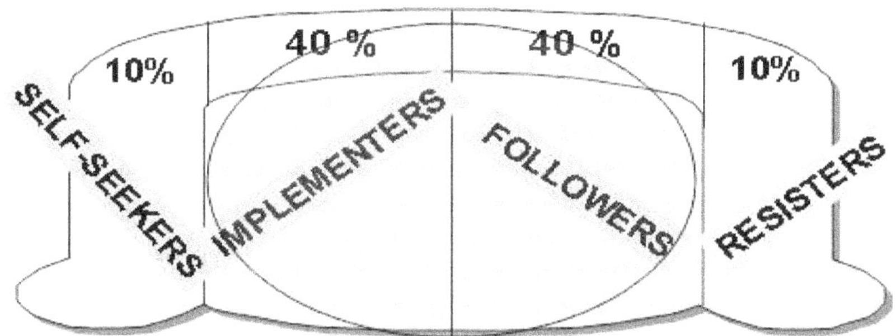

SELF SEEKERS- HIGHLY MOTIVATED- SELF INTEREST
IMPLEMENTERS – MOTIVATED-COMMUNITY MINDED
FOLLOWERS – MOTIVATABLE-COMMUNITY MINDED
RESISTERS – REJECT YOU [ROM 11:11]

We ought to keep in mind that we are not abandoning or giving up on the Resisters. It might be said that we are *postponing* them. The apostle Paul came to a point where he said he was forsaking his efforts among his fellow Jews because of their resistance and was therefore going over to the Gentiles, to make his fellow Jews *"jealous."* In his confidence, his reasoning was that the Resisters would be induced to forsake their stubbornness once they observed the positive outcomes of the development activity that was being undertaken by the others.

It could be possible that when the Resisters observe the positive results being accomplished among the implementers and followers, with agents facilitating their improvement and working toward their success, they too might become desirous and motivated to participate in the development efforts out of envy.

During a trip to India, the overseer of a slum area heard of my presence in the vicinity and invited me to visit his compound. He had resigned his position as a corporate electrical engineer and dedicated himself to working with the slum dwellers.

I was astonished at his work. He had a clothing distribution outlet, a small medical and first aid clinic, a small but successful school and literacy program, a food kitchen and pantry all successfully organized and developed by himself with much of his own personal wealth. It was hard to understand why he wanted to see me when I should have been learning from him. I was puzzled, humbled, and intimidated. Nonetheless, he wanted my advice.

He shared his frustration over what he called this tiny group of "interlopers" in the slum. They were continually in the forefront of any new initiatives he wanted to undertake and were constantly at his door seeking favors. They were a constant source of irritation to himself and the other dwellers because of their aggressiveness and self-interest. They were always the same people. He wanted my advice as to what to do about them.

I drew him the above sketch of the four personality types and asked if in some way it fit his dilemma with his "interlopers." He said it matched his situation perfectly. When I asked what he did with them he said he barred them from taking part in any of the activities of the slum but that it was filling him with guilt and sadness. He didn't know what to do.

My only suggestion was that he considers his options to work with the "interlopers" (Self Seekers) and realize that it requires patience and firmness to motivate them toward generosity, selflessness, and greater regard for the community. If this group can be encouraged and mentored to be more charitable toward their neighbors under the principle of "to whom much is given, much is required," this group could be a potential, wholesome source of future leaders for the community. Mentoring them would take great patience and determination but could have positive results. Otherwise, they probably will remain a heavy risk to community harmony.

CHAPTER NINE: *LIVING LIFE WITH THEM*

Community development workers clearly need to understand the different roles they will be called on to play in enhancing the community development process.

ROLES OF A COMMUNITY DEVELOPER WORKER

1) IDENTIFIER - If we expect to be successful in working with groups, we need to identify with the people in as many ways possible. Learning the customs and culture of the group and adapting to its lifestyle and even taking on some of its characteristics can be critical to our success. Otherwise, we may forever be considered an outsider and will be treated as such.

> 1 COR 9:20-23 - *"To the Jews, I became like a Jew, to win the Jews. To those under the law, I became like one under the law (though I myself am not under the law), so as to win those under the law. To those not having the law I became like one not having the law (though I am not free from God's law but am under Christ's law), so as to win those not having the law. To the weak, I became weak to win the weak. I have become all things to all men so that by all possible means I might save some. I do all this for the sake of the Gospel that I might share in its blessings."* NIV
>
> When Jesus came to earth, He went to every possible length to become "like us." He identified with us to experience life with us.
>
> HEB 2:17-18 - *"For this reason He had to be made like His brothers in every way, in order that He might become a merciful and faithful high priest in service to God and that He might make atonement for the sins of the people. Because He himself suffered when He was tempted, He is able to help those who are being tempted."* NIV

FITTING IN - To enter in to any social order is a challenge that can be accomplished only with a decision of our wills. We must make a decision to be adaptable and flexible to things new, strange, puzzling or even annoying. The ability to get along in strange situations takes great humility and wisdom, tact, prudence, discretion and discernment.

To be effective, fitting in and getting along needs to take pre-eminence over one's rights and preferences and even one's individuality. In some cultures, women wearing lipstick, rouge or mascara are pre-judged to be loose living and promiscuous. Hiking shorts on a hot day may be comfortable but in some cultures, shorts other than at home are frowned upon. Westerners (Americans too) overseas, commonly insensitive to anything like cultural differences, are often considered to be of an inferior culture because of the lack of sensitivity to the cultural or social customs of the host nation.

WHEN YOU'RE THE OUTSIDER, IT'S UP TO YOU. The final responsibility in getting along with your host group is yours. If we expect our hosts to meet our needs according to our own tastes and preferences, we can communicate a haughtiness and arrogance that will limit our acceptability and hinder our effectiveness. If you don't make the effort to blend in, you'll quickly be considered an outsider to the detriment of your work and success. At its worst, your host group will try to figure out how to avoid you or be rid of you.

We're most often alienated because we bring in our own notions of how things ought to be and then we're disappointed when situations don't match our expectations. We might develop fears that our needs won't be met and display irritation, often visible to our hosts and hostesses. Human nature is such that there will be times when our own particular preferences don't seem to be that unreasonable or demanding, yet of necessity, we are forced to put up with cultural situations that do seem unreasonable.

Being flexible takes preeminence over one's own individuality, preferences, and rights in adapting to a different culture. Guard against high expectations. Don't expect results too quickly. Don't dwell on failures.

If we want to be effective, we ought to learn to lay aside and not brood over disappointments. Releasing disappointments frees us from negative attitudes that could hinder us in forming necessary, successful relationships in our host environment.

In the Desert Storm operation of 1991, having been relocated to the various Middle-Eastern nations in the war with Iraq, Western and American servicemen and women were confronted with different standards of modesty, manners, inter-personal relating between the sexes and personal behavior. Issues of cultural offenses were arising to such a pitch and with such frequency that most Americans received primer courses on the subject and received crash courses in cultural sensitivity.

The fact that so many Americans were making supreme sacrifices and the United States was spending billions of dollars on behalf of countries in that region in their defense, allowed military personnel no privileged exemption from expected compliance with the cultural norms and customs.

WAYS TO IDENTIFY

a) LANGUAGE - It is extremely complimentary to a people when we make every effort to speak their language, even in part. It is a terrible testimony to expect or demand that they speak our language if we're the outsider. Yet that is what many of us do. If we trivialize the importance of learning the language in a foreign culture, we can risk hurting our effectiveness in our work.

We had a young Canadian named Steve on our team in Guam who, as part of his assigned ministry, directed the youth group at a small, local Filipino church. As a special occasion, the church was going to celebrate its anniversary with a fiesta of music, food, fellowship and speeches. For that anniversary occasion, in their honor, Steve began to learn a little folk song in Tagalog, the dialect of the people's national language. I remember overhearing him practicing in his room and other places as I walked by. He did not play a guitar very well but he knew a few chords and he practiced a lot. During the fiesta celebration, Steve performed his little song to the delight and giggles of the crowd as he made an occasional mistake in pronunciation or his accent. He gamely and respectfully got through the song and received a spirited ovation.

Many months later, when Steve came to the end of his term, it was time for him to return home. It seemed the whole church, men women and children came to see him off at the airport.

As he walked toward the departure gate, Steve was altogether covered with flower leis from his chin, neck, shoulders, and both arms. As he reached the exit door, he turned to us and with one arm all draped with the leis, gave a big, swooping, final, farewell wave. He turned and exited through the door.

He may not know it to this day, but as Steve was waving goodbye to us in the terminal, I happened to look at the church crowd around me and saw that most of the men, women, and children had tears in their eyes.

Later, on several occasions, when I would meet up with any of the church members in town we would eventually get around to reminiscing about Steve.

We shared many memories. The thing they remembered most about him was that occasion when he sang that little folk song to them in their language at their church celebration.

When you leave a place of ministry, wouldn't you like to leave like that - men, women, and children weeping at your departure? Language is important. In seeking to identify with the people, we need to remember that learning their language can be critical. We may struggle at it and make mistakes, but they will be forgiving at the genuine sincerity of effort.

b) FOOD - A young missionary trainee, who as a visitor to a family in a foreign country, when the food was placed before her at mealtime exclaimed, "Yukl"

It was hardly the way to exercise manners, let alone win endearing friends whom we're trying to please.

It is an amazing thing how food is such an area of concern for people around the world. It's pretty safe to say that, of all our ethno-centric cultural preferences, the one that we seem to be most possessive of is food. We simply have a hard time adjusting to changes in our eating habits and food selections.

Overseas, people often expect that food will be an area of potential complaint for visitors who come to their country. Perhaps they learned from experience that most visitors will find complaint or something objectionable in the local food. Westerners, Americans among them, can be most demanding and less than charitable in expectations of having needs met. Nowhere is it more evident than in the area of food.

Preparing and serving food is not simply a functional duty but an extension of the host's hospitality. It is an extension of themselves. They are, in fact, offering their sensitive care for a visitor's enjoyment. Most are eager to please and can easily observe telltale signs of the visitor's dissatisfaction. Indifference or any sign of disapproval of their efforts is hurtful and can be damaging to the relationship.

Yet there is great reward in bonding and relationship building by simply receiving, accepting, and partaking of the food that is available and served to us. Most often, it comes with nutritional, delectable, and surprisingly enjoyable taste experiences if we give it a chance. Being adventuresome in new tasting experiences can be fun.

Small and gracious but sincere compliments over food can go a long way in fostering needed friendships. We should never underestimate the value of mealtimes or fellowship times over food in helping us to relate and identify with people.

c) LIFESTYLE - In identifying with a people, learn to cope with the unusual in the whole area of their customs and cultural habits. It may have to do with type of housing, toilet facilities, wearing apparel, transportation, relations between the sexes, forms of humor, treatment of elders and children, to body language and facial expression.

When traveling overseas, if we want to be sensitive to the culture, we'll need to be conscious of modesty and appropriate apparel standards. Taboos often occur in the areas of men's and women's attire as to what may be considered acceptable in business or even casual dress. Although widely accepted in Western cultures, in some cultures, sports-type shorts, for example, are not considered appropriate attire. In public, men are expected to wear long trousers and women dresses or skirt type apparel.

Trying to assimilate and identify with people in under-developed or emerging nations can be especially challenging, especially if we ourselves are from a developed nation. Housing may be somewhat rudimentary and unsophisticated with limited plumbing or simple or even crude toilet facilities. Being flexible and adaptable is essential to win and enjoy the acceptance of the people. Identifying with the people is simply experiencing life with them as they know it and live it. Take risks, avoid fears, learn by doing, go for it.

Doing research on the customs and culture of our host community is essential for successful acculturation in identifying with the people whose acceptance we covet.

d) WORK - Find ways to do physical work with the people, otherwise they'll always treat you like a guest and you may never be close to them.

When introducing my future bride, who is German, to my extended family that is Polish at a family house party, she was extremely nervous such that it was difficult for her to relax. To calm her nerves, I suggested she find ways to help in the kitchen among the ladies of the family, like cutting veggies, putting frosting on the cake or filling the water glasses. She did that and was instantly embraced by my very ethnic family, despite the differences in our cultural backgrounds. It was a sharing-of-work principle that somehow bonds us to others quickly. Needless to say, she received instant acceptance by all the members of my family.

Finding ways to work among the people will build relationships quickly.

e) MAKE A FRIEND - Find a "bridge" person as someone who will be open enough with you as a friend to help you learn about the culture. They can coach you, alert you to cultural mistakes, help you with the language, give advice and help you along with adapting to the culture.

Bruce Olson dedicated his book *Bruchko* to Bobarishora (Bobby) and has a chapter dedicated to his "Pact Brother." Bobby became Bruce's best friend and bridge person, giving him great insight into the customs, and culture of the hill tribe Motilone Indians of Colombia. Bobby facilitated Bruce's successful adaptation to the culture which paved the way for Bruce to lead the Motilones in their eventual conversion to Christianity from a warlike people to the most developed hill tribe people in the world.[13]

Make a friend in the culture.

CAUTION: Though we may make many cultural mistakes, we ought not to despair. Don't try too hard. Don't over-identify to a point of looking obviously silly. You can make yourself an object of derision. Be assured that there is distinctiveness about you.

A Chinese friend in Singapore, when I expressed my failures and frustrations in always trying to do the culturally appropriate thing, consoled me with these remarks: *"Joe, we realize that you are a Westerner. It is very obvious. We know you come from a different culture and that you can't automatically know our ways. What we are looking at is the heart. We are asking ourselves, 'Can I relate to this person? Is this person really sincere? Does this person have integrity?'"*

So even in what may be our dismal cultural performance, there is still room for matters of the heart. We need always to try our best in humility, but certainly not despair or give up at our mistakes and failures.

ROLES OF A COMMUNITY DEVELOPER WORKER CONT'D

2) BE AN OBSERVER - What are we to observe? Through simple observation, we can determine what kind and levels of development the community has underway. Again **LUKE 2:52** becomes a useful aid in observing community life.

Committing our observations to memory so as to record them afterward in journals or diaries for permanent reference is a good practice. For example, on day one, we can ask ourselves what is going on in the area of *mental development* – day two, in *physical development* and day three, in *spiritual development,* and so on.

---

13 Bruce E. Olson, Bruchko, (Altamonte Springs, FL: Creation House, 1978) p.113-118

Focus on routines, incidents, and problems - not only on what you see but also on what you don't see. Use your five senses. Do not walk around with a notebook like an official doing an investigation. Make it an adventure. Be cool and relax.

Worldwide, in every culture there are positive customs and habits and ungodly ones - even destructive ones. For genuine relationship building, affirm what's good in the culture. For example, *"I admire the way you treat the elderly"* or *"your young people are well behaved".*

What's neutral, leave alone. Don't be insincere or patronizing. Do not use a slash and burn approach when you see something ungodly. What's bad, wait and plan how you can discuss the issue with the appropriate leaders at a later time.

PROV 15:28 - "*the heart of the righteous studies how to answer....*" NKJV-OB

3) LEARNER - Emphasize being a receiver rather than a provider. Balance receiving information about the people and how they live their lives rather than presuming how to improve them. Learn from their attempts at self-sufficiency. Ask questions! Listen! We will want to build on what they know. We can learn what they know by *observation*, by them volunteering information and us asking them questions.

Learn about the area when possible through research, reports, journals, and records of its history. When possible become familiar with leaders and seek interviews. Building on what they know is a principle in development.

(It is also a key method in evangelism. In ACTS 8:26 Philip started his commentary at the point where the Ethiopian had his question.)

Learn by asking questions to find their starting point to build on what they know!

(There is some caution to be used in asking questions since in some cultures it can be offensive to ask "direct" questions. Asking questions in a gentle, civil manner is far more effective than asking in an aggressive, impulsive or threatening manner. Damaging questions can also be in the form of asking about their "needs" as they might presume you are interested in filling those needs.)

GIFT GIVING

(OR BRINGING UNWANTED DEVELOPMENT)

DID YOU EVER RECEIVE A GIFT YOU DIDN'T WANT?

You may have wanted it to be an act of kindness, but your gift was not appreciated or may have even hurt the relationship through an unintended offense.

Often we do things or give gifts from an imperfect consideration. In our own way, we decide the person or group would like what we're giving. It pleases us to think we've been kind and generous. But they may not have desired the gift which is why they don't use it or keep it. Without sensitively doing a little research or investigation as to their wants or preferences, we give from an imperfect view that pleases us as the givers. We are not really attempting to please the receiver according to their hopes, desires, or aspirations but make assumptions based on our own likes.

We do the same with the poor in development. We presume the help we're giving them is what they need or should have according to our choices and decisions. It turns out that our decisions and gifts may be an imposition on them. We give gifts that they may not really want. They may show appreciation and defer to us, but in their hearts, they don't really want it. Thus, it goes unused and perhaps even discarded or falls into disrepair. So our gift is pleasing ourselves but not necessarily the receivers.

With this in mind, we come to the most difficult role of the community development worker – *"Needs Assessor."*

4) NEEDS ASSESSOR

(We offer a cautionary note here. From experience, we've learned that most of us usually "identify" problems in view of the "solution" we bring. If our personal specialty is medical, we'll see the medical needs. If our specialty is sanitation and water, we'll see the sanitation problems. It is human nature for us to define and emphasize problems according to our own specialty concentration. We need to guard against our own subjective focus.)

A community development worker will be more successful by adopting a "generalist" way of observing and assessing needs. It helps us to be more objective in focusing and determining the most urgent needs, rather than automatically defaulting to our own specialty skill.

Assessing needs is the most difficult area of community development. Often, it can happen that the people already know what they want to see changed. We may likely be catalysts or facilitators for what is truly in their hearts. The ideal is to motivate and facilitate them to make decisions on what they prefer to see changed, in what direction, and with what resources. The people may not always be right, but agreement could lead to later changes on other needs. Good people skills are helpful in this area.

There is the story of the young missionary who embedded in a village and after following all the protocols and good sense of identifying with the people and gaining their trust, felt some urgency that the village had a high infant mortality rate. Many children were dying before they were two years old at an unusually high rate due to various childhood diseases. His assessment was that with a small clinic doing small training programs and vaccination procedures they could reduce that figure to less alarming levels.

In a quiet moment with the chief, he broached the subject of developing and building a small first aid or medical clinic. Without hesitation, the chief dismissed the idea. The missionary nightly began to pray that the Lord would change the mind of the chief to see the advantages of the clinic especially since there was news spreading that a measles outbreak was occurring in the countryside. On bringing up the subject a second time, the chief was still adamant and stated that the village didn't need a clinic, it needed a soccer field. The missionary was aghast at the seeming unreasonable trade-off.

He continued to ask the Lord to change the mind of the chief to plan a clinic. Instead, to his surprise, he felt the message from the Lord through prayer was to agree with the chief on the soccer field.

So they went through the process with the missionary facilitating land acquisition, borrowing equipment for tree, shrub, and foliage removal, and organizing work parties with the villagers for land clearance. It seems the whole village participated.

On the day of its opening, the villagers christened the field and organized a huge inaugural celebration with food, music, games and all kinds of festivities. Sitting together and observing the celebration, the chief turned to the missionary and said, "Se*e I told you we needed a soccer field. My people are coming together again. They are working together and smiling and laughing again!... So tell me, what do you think we should do next?"* The missionary sheepishly responded, *"Well chief, there is this matter of the medical clinic."* The chief said, *"Good idea. We must protect the children."*

Three Important Factors In Assessing The Needs Of A Community:

a) THE PEOPLE - Whose agenda and whose decisions will we follow? Will the people be the active subjects of development or will they be the passive objects of development and possibly victims of our impositions?

People probably already know what they want to see changed and we may simply accelerate what's in their hearts. We may have the tendency to identify problems from what we perceive as "needs" while the people may be identifying problems from their perspective of "hopes."

Assessing people's needs should be a shared process as determined by talks with the people, interviews in the community, research, formal and informal surveys, prayer and intercession, and observation.

At a conference, I had the experience of meeting a young missionary who was working arduously among the river people in the Amazon region of Brazil. He was one of the most committed and likeable missionaries I ever met. He sought the meeting with me when he heard of my interest in community development.

Getting to his point during our conversation, he challenged me with the statement that he didn't believe community development works. He said he and his team had tried as many as seven different community projects with the people along the Amazon and none of them ever worked. He briefly described their attempts and the resulting failures. Then brashly he said, "Now, you tell me in one sentence why our projects didn't work."

Still knowing very little of his story and of what his team really attempted, he wanted me to tell him the reasons for their failures in one sentence? I was startled by his audacity.

As is my custom in predicaments like that, I bowed my head and quickly muttered a prayer under my nose something like, "Lord, you need to give answer to this young man." I took a deep breath and this is what I said, "your projects didn't work because you probably never asked the people."

It seemed the flesh on his face began to droop while his head began to hang low and helpless. The power of the truth in that statement hit him pretty hard. In all their sincere and noble attempts to help, his team had never consulted the people as to what they might have wanted to see changed. In essence, the people felt the projects belonged to the missionaries and so they never took ownership of what was going on. With time, all the team's efforts failed.

In another instance, in one of the Marianas Islands in the West Pacific, a young missionary team wanted to install an underground pipeline to a village from a tapped water-spring up a hill. It was to alleviate the burden on the women who had to cart the water in heavy containers from up the hill back down to their village homes for their use. The team was going to install this project for the village people and even brought all their own food and supplies. The project would take some weeks.

During the course of digging the trenches, installation, and burying the pipeline, some team members took ill, including the one who had the most plumbing experience. They began to suffer delays. The team began to run short of food . At the same time, the team wondered why the village people didn't join in to help on the project. The delays led to something of a crisis for the team as they ran out of food and became exhausted from the work.

Finally, after a signal from the chief, the village people began to help with the installation and donated food to the team. The project finally came to an end and the team returned home to their neighboring island.

About a year and a half later, some of the team returned to check on the pipeline project and, to their dismay, they found it in total disrepair. Some of the pipeline in several areas had become uncovered from the soil and vehicular traffic of all sorts ran over the piping and crushed it causing it to leak and rendered it unusable. The villagers never undertook repairs because they looked upon the pipeline as belonging to the missionaries and so expected them to come back to repair it. The village chief had never been consulted and so the people never took ownership of the project. They were never included. Even so, the villagers had no supplies or ways to acquire materials to make the necessary repairs and so the project was really abandoned.

In a similar situation in St. Lucia, in the Caribbean, a huge church building had half of its roof blown off during a violent storm. For months, when it would rain during church services, the people would sit on that side of the building which was covered by the remaining roof while the rain simply poured down into the church on the other side. When I asked why the people didn't fix the roof but allowed that situation to continue, they said that the church was built by visiting missionaries and so they expected the missionaries to come back to fix it.

The missionaries never consulted the people as to what kind of building they would like, how it should be outfitted or even as to its location. Even though they were now using it, the people never took ownership of the church. They did not see it as "their" church because they were never consulted as to any aspect of its construction and thus believed it was still the missionaries' church.

WHEN THE PEOPLE HAVE A VOICE:

BHOOMI SENNA MOVEMENT- INDIA

INTERVIEW:

Q. "In what sense do you think outside help is useful?"

A. "We need outside help for analysis and understanding of our situation and experience but not for telling us what to do. An outsider who comes with ready - made solutions and advice is worse than useless. He must first understand from us what our questions are, and help us articulate our questions better, and then help us find solutions. Outsiders also have to change. He alone is friend who helps us think about our problems on our own.

from DEVELOPMENT: SEEDS OF CHANGE[14]

DISCUSS: THE BOOMHI SENNA STATEMENT

b) STRATEGIC - Another key consideration in assessing needs is that our efforts be *strategic* in that they are a result of *planning* with clear-cut objectives. Our goals initially are to meet "felt needs" that are causing some kind of burden on the people. A felt need is one that is threatening or causing the people some kind of stress or pressure. Our overall objective in bringing development is to meet a felt-need in a meaningful way.

MEETING A "FELT" NEED

Success is really measured by how it changes the community for the better. For success in meeting a felt need does it - - -

- Fit local patterns? - Does it harmonize with the local cultural norms or will it impact the culture harmfully?

- Benefit the poor or the already prosperous? - Is it going to enhance the opportunities for the ones we're really trying to reach? Is whatever effort we're undergoing easily duplicate-able?

- Use local resources? - Wherever possible we want to use resources the Lord has invested in that community. We want to acquire materials and needed supplies locally, when possible, to aid local industries and businesses.

---

14 Author and source unknown except for caption citing DEVELOPMENT: SEEDS OF CHANGE

- Employ people rather than displaces them? - Bringing high technology and equipment usually helps only a few, while others are made idle and become observers. We want to allow opportunity for everyone to benefit.

Use tools, equipment, and technologies with which the people are familiar and that are appropriate to the local level. When possible, they should be only moderately advanced from local levels so as not to displace someone from a work opportunity.[15]

c) SMALL - The advantages of starting small are enormous. The poor often lack experience, organization and confidence in large-scale undertakings. In bringing change, we want to start small with something simple, not too complex, and not too long to achieve. We want a quick success.

A quick success will raise the people's confidence particularly if they struggle with low self-esteem. If we start with something too complex or too long in duration to accomplish, we may reinforce the people's notion of themselves that they can' t do it. We want to build on what they already know and something with which they are familiar. Starting with something simple that is low risk and requires limited technology will enhance our potential for a quick success.

Marsha in Australia told the story of Charmaine, a single mother of three, who was despondent over the abandonment by her husband. Charmaine was in complete lethargy as reflected in her totally neglected housekeeping. When Marsha politely suggested that Charmaine make an effort to clean up her house as a positive creative act, Charmaine broke down in tears. She was unable to cope with undertaking what to her was so daunting a task. Marsha suggested then just to clean the kitchen. Again, Charmaine broke into tears. Marsha suggested cleaning up the bedroom. Again, Charmaine couldn't cope.

Finally, Marsha suggested that Charmaine begin by just cleaning up the top of her dresser. After a pause, Charmaine felt she could do that and consented. Then she cleaned the top of her desk, then the top of the chest of drawers and step by step, little by little, Charmaine finally cleaned up her bedroom. From that small beginning, Charmaine started on a path to take control of her life to where she now sells small arts and crafts to support herself and her children.

15 Several of the ideas expressed here are expansions of principles advocated by Roland Bunch in Two Ears of Corn (Oklahoma City, Oklahoma: World Neighbors 1982)

ROLES OF DEVELOPMENT WORKER CONT'D.

5) INFORMATIONER

***[BE A* GATHERER]**

In attempting to bring development, following the good sense of identifying with the people and experiencing life with them, our top priority is to acquire as much information about the community as possible. We want to make a reasonable determination as to how to proceed. Some knowledge of all aspects of community life is essential if we want to avoid a hasty and misguided plan.

[BE A BRINGER] –

Be slow in bringing information and in making suggestions or giving advice. We do not want to appear to be an "expert," such that people will look to us not only to identify their problems but then also to bring the solutions. That could start us on the road to dependency. The preferred approach is to help the people discover the problems by themselves and lead them to solutions.

Development work is often based on the misconception that if we plan enough things to happen, change is sure take place. The major contributing factor in development is what people believe about the way things are. If they believe their situation is normal they may not want to change. Often it is most urgent that the people be led to discover they have a problem because they may believe and accept their backward situation as "normal."

There is the story of the village chief who felt that the chickens dying in his village was a more critical problem than the children dying at an early age at a very high rate. He felt that the children dying at that high rate of morbidity had been going on for years and therefore considered that situation "normal." The fact that the chickens were dying was a new and unusual condition, and since it had never happened before, was a matter of greater concern.

A C.D. worker in Mexico set up a microscope in the center of a village for people to see samples of the river water which the people used for their water needs. When the people saw for themselves the polluted water they were feeding their babies that was causing so much stomach distress they stopped bathing their animals in the river and began boiling their water.

In the final analysis, community development is setting in motion a sequence of changes that takes place in the people toward their development. We rarely go from point A to point B, like so:

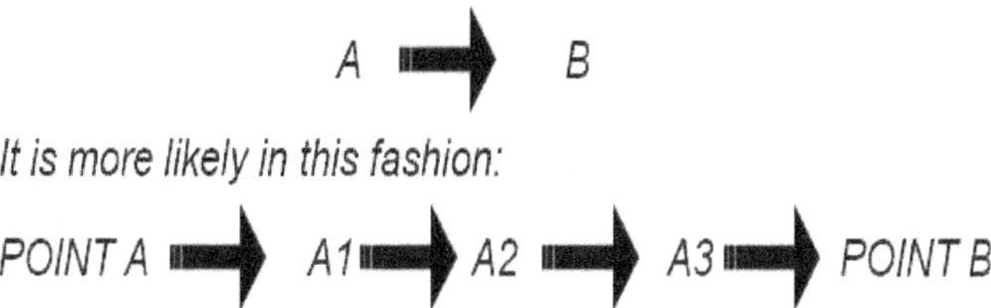

The first change that must take place is in....information. Change must take place first in the thinking of the people, and that's through information.

To coin a term, ***awaretization*** is a process of helping people recognize their problems and the opportunities within their reach. Making them aware is critical. If they don't believe they have a problem, they will not be motivated to take action. They are most easily moved when experiencing dissatisfaction of some kind or stress or in a period of transition of some type.

To illustrate the point of how the change process occurs, I'm reminded of the incidents in my life that lead to my spiritual conversion to become a Bible believing Christian.

At a time in a park, an eighteen-year-old red headed young lady was doing some personal evangelism. As I ignored her approaches, she in turn called me a "sinner." That call-out irritated me as I passed by. I thought of myself as a fairly good person, a churchgoer, generally kind, true to my family and friends, with the other common, decent qualities attributed to most people.

But her claim disconcerted me and, over time, caused me to ponder what it was she had alleged. She had challenged my thinking. That set me on a pilgrimage seeking to clarify the kind of person I was to a point where I recognized that despite my career success, material acquisitions, and my high feelings about myself, there was a deep emptiness I had inside.

Sometime later, at a social / business meeting of believers and non-believers, my journey culminated in my positive response to an invitation from my boss and business partner to become a Christian and obedient follower of Jesus Christ. From that point on, my whole life changed. Three years later, I resigned all my positions in the company and left with my family for the mission field. The whole process of my conversion began with a simple change in my thinking - someone had called me a sinner. Then, with time, there was a whole sequence of changes in what I thought and believed about things up to my decision to become a believer.

IN PRINCIPLE, MOST LIFE CHANGING EXPERIENCES OCCUR

1) at a recognized need or a problem
2) when held values are challenged
3) in a social, caring, concerned context (community)
4) after a period of reflection
5) with a resulting change in behavior

Community development is setting in motion a sequence of changes with the first change taking place in...information. The second major change that must occur is in what the people believe about their situation. If their beliefs change then their behavior will change. Our ultimate objective is the change in their behavior. When their behavior changes development will be underway.

The way we change might be illustrated by something called the K.A.P. system.

K - KNOWLEDGE – A change in their facts (mind)

A - ATTITUDE – A change in their beliefs (heart)

P - PRACTICES - A change in their behavior (actions)

Without a change in all three areas and especially in behavior, change be temporary and superficial.

Schematically we can illustrate change this way:

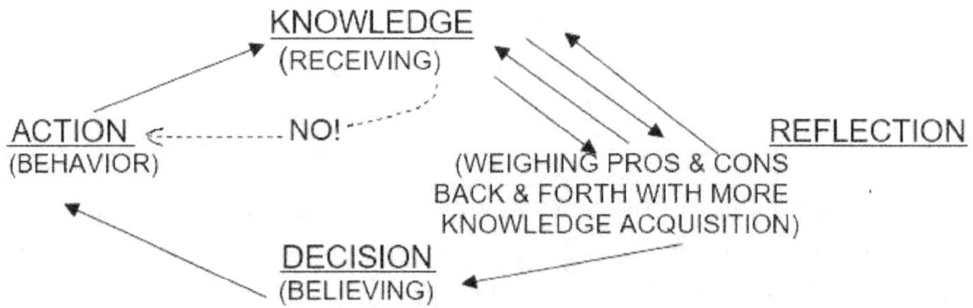

The illustration shows how we as individuals change. With the new knowledge (facts), we go through a process of reflection. Reflection is healthy in that the individual determines the value of what is being considered, counting the cost and perhaps rebounding for more facts and knowledge before making a final determination. Once we take ownership of that decision, our whole behavior will change.

Reflection is a key to bringing change. Often, if we go directly from knowledge to action, without reflection, our decision can be hasty and impulsive resulting in an unsupported decision, possibly leading to recantation or backsliding later. In my own evangelism efforts, I feel liberated in the sense that I can see the wisdom of giving individuals time and space for reflection to make their own decision to follow Jesus. I no longer feel disappointment if they do not make an immediate decision at my witness, as I know that through reflection their decision will be strengthened as they take ownership of it.[16]

We were doing an open-air evangelism outreach with my team in Seoul, South Korea outside of a shopping/theater district that was closing down for the night. The crowds were streaming by as others gathered around us in earnest. I gave a message on how we could be world changers if we would first change our hearts.

Following my message, as our team mingled with the crowd, I noticed a young man standing off to the side with an obvious desire to speak to me. I called him over and through a translator, he told me about his roommate at the university who was a very devout Christian. He said he admired his roommate very much and had a deep respect for him as a model of living out his faith. But he had some questions that were puzzling him and in his culture, it would have been disrespectful to ask his roommate those direct and possibly hostile questions. As I was an obvious foreigner preaching the message, he felt the liberty to take this chance to ask me the questions that were troubling him.

It was at the time of the unfortunate, serious scandals of two very prominent television evangelists in the United States that gained worldwide attention. The young Korean asked how I could continue to remain a Christian when our leaders were falling into such scandal and disrepute. He thought it was being hypocritical to belong to a religion when such things were happening to some of our most respected and popular leaders.

As I've done before, I quietly muttered a prayer for the Lord to give answer to this young man. Finally, this is what I said, "What happened to those men is another reminder of how weak we are and why we need the Lord. It reminds us of how we can fail and why we need His power and strength. We don't follow those men, we follow Jesus. Jesus is our model. We look to Him for wisdom, guidance and direction for our lives. Those men are meant to give us teaching and encouragement but they are not our model. Jesus is our model and the One we follow."

With my answer, the young man became quiet.

After a brief moment, I asked if he had any more questions.

He said "No."

---

16 Several ideas mentioned here are expansions on basic principles imparted by Dr. D. Merrill Ewert, Principles of Community Development, (Wheaton Illinois: Wheaton College, c.1987)

I said, "Well then, do you want to become a Christian?"

He said, "No, but now.... I want to think about it."

With his new information and insight, the young Korean wanted to go through his own period of reflection...... *"now I want to think about it."*

It's good to give people time and space to go through a period of reflection to take full ownership of their decision.

PROV 19:2-3 - *"It is not good to have zeal without knowledge nor to be hasty and miss the way. A man's own folly ruins his life, yet his heart rages against the Lord."* **NIV**

In ACTS 17:11, the Berean's did not take Paul's word for what he was preaching. They wanted to see for themselves if what he was saying was true. They wanted to go through their own period of reflection. Paul does not call them doubters, scoffers, or skeptics, he calls them noble-minded.

REFLECTION TO BRING CHANGE IS VITAL:

1) the people take control of their thinking

2) they become responsible for their own thinking

3) they come to recognize their problems by themselves

4) they discover the solutions by themselves

5) they will believe they've done it by themselves.

At some point, we will be information *Bringers*. If we are too assertive with advice and information we will risk appearing as experts and limit our effectiveness in helping the people develop. We want to see the people grow and develop to take control of their own lives and outcomes and not risk leading them into dependency.

This creates a dilemma for us in how best to transmit information without appearing to be an expert.

HOW WE TRANSMIT INFORMATION WILL BE CRITICAL.

The most cautious way to bring information without appearing to be an expert is to help people discover the answer by themselves. We do this best by ***asking questions*** about their situations. Asking them questions stimulates an inductive learning process whereby they can be led to a conclusion.

The Lord did this with Adam in the garden after he and Eve fell into disobedience. In GEN 3:9-13, although omniscient in His powers, God nevertheless asks Adam a series of questions, not because He doesn't know, but to stimulate Adam to reflect on his situation and come to a realization of the seriousness of what he had done. Asking questions is a very effective means of transmitting information. It's God's method to stimulate people to discover the answer by themselves.

Asking questions in an inoffensive way is a skill that ought to be developed. In some cultures, it can be considered impolite or rude to ask direct questions so attention must be paid to the manner of posing the questions. For example, instead of asking an individual how many brothers and sisters they have, asking if they come from a large family is more polite. That gives them the freedom to expand and tell specifically the number of brothers and sisters they have if they so choose. Instead of asking "why?" questions, we might ask what the meaning or significance is of a situation or action. Being less direct is less offensive. But asking questions to lead people to discover the answer is very effective and should be utilized.

In transmitting information, it is helpful to ***contextualize*** the information by using appropriate communication skills. Use of culturally familiar metaphors, storytelling, even parables can be very effective is communicating information which the listener can apprehend and remember. Jesus did this when He talked of rocks and stones and wheat and tares. We need to achieve clarity in our communications using all possible means to ensure the people can relate to and understand our message

Using ***frequent repetition*** in transmitting information with as many media as possible, to appeal to as many senses as possible, is a great help especially where illiteracy is a problem. Lectures, organized group discussion, posters, slogans, other readings, film strips, field trips are all aids to transmitting information especially in casting vision for improvement and to stimulate participation.

TYPES OF QUESTIONS:

GEN 3:9-13, 4:1-10, MATT 16:13-20, LUKE 7:36-50, 10:25-37, 24:13-35

- *a) BSERVATION - WHAT? HOW MANY? WHAT ARE THEY DOING?*
- *b) REFLECTION - WHAT'S IT MEAN?*
- *c) PROBING - WHAT ARE THE IMPLICATIONS?*
- *d) APPLICATION - WHAT ARE YOU GOING TO DO ABOUT IT?*

ROLES OF A COMMUNITY DEVELOPMENT WORKER CONT'D.

6) FACILITATOR - (FACILE – EASY)

2 COR 1:24 - *"Domineering over your faith is not my purpose. I prefer to work with you toward your happiness."* **NAB**

Paul declares the real vision of the facilitator is not to seek control over the people or to dominate but to work with them for their benefit.

The following skills can be acquired and rehearsed although often they can be personal giftings. These skills are very useful in dealing with groups.

SKILLS OF THE FACILITATOR

A) MOTIVATOR - stimulates choices and actions for the people's benefit that makes them feel good about themselves - offers solutions not just advice. Opposite to manipulation - which makes people feel bad about themselves

B) INTEGRATOR - weaves a planned secondary impact along with the primary impact. Weaves inputs from the community with his own input. Weaves together ethical and spiritual content along with the physical, intellectual and social activities of development. Weaves in basic levels of development with envisioned future higher levels of development.

C) MODELER - Good modeling exhibits good action before giving advice, suggestion or teaching. According to Acts 1:1, Jesus "did" and "taught" these things. Other biblical admonitions: "blessed is he" ...who "practices" and " teaches" MATT 5:19. Ezra set his heart on the "study" and "practice" of the law of the Lord and to "teaching" - EZRA 7:10

Of special concern to the Christian is the reality that one is a model whether one is aware of it or not, whether one likes it or not. Christians are always modeling their attitudes, values, language, and their behavior for better or worse.

D) ENABLER - facilitates the people in what they must have and know to take action. People must be afforded training or some instruction for tasks they are expected to perform along with the proper tools or equipment to get the job done. Basically, there are two types of enablers – one is a *performer,* who prefers to perform the action himself while others watch to learn.

A *transformer* follows a simple but effective strategy of training with a hands-on , joint approach between instructor and learner - "I do- you watch" ; "we do - we watch" ; "you do - I watch." the process of working through the instruction together produces quicker and more tangible results.

In addition, not hoarding our abilities but making every effort to transmit them to others is an appreciated act of kindness. Don't hoard your abilities, give them away – pass them on to others. Teaching is a biblical expectation of true leaders. 1 PET 4:10 - *"Each one should use the gift he has received to serve others, faithfully administering God's grace in its various forms."* NIV

E) MOBILIZER - is a motivator except that instead on working within one group, a mobilizer organizes and coordinates several groups to action.

F) NETWORKER - Networking is a computer term that implies making helpful connections between people-to-people, people to information, and people to supplies. It may even imply connecting people to your notes. Don't hoard your ministry, as with your skills, give them away.

G) EVALUATOR - Monitoring progress of projects or individuals is essential. Periodic reviews of progress in order to make adjustments are not only wise they are also protective. Do not wait until the end of a project to make modifications - it's too late. Criticism after the project is finished or complaints about performance when completed can be a great discouragement to workers.

H) RELEASER - seeks to release people to their gifts and abilities and their full potential in God. A releaser is eager to nurture and elevate people to higher levels of authority and responsibility and, of whom it can be said, seeks to work himself out of a job.

(Releasing others to responsibility does have some qualifiers in that the people ought to have a certain level of maturity. We know from the book of Job that maturity does not necessarily depend on age but on noble character, commitment, faithfulness, a teachable spirit and readiness to obey.

(Releasing people too soon to responsibility can be an abdication which may not be helpful.)

AS FACILITATORS, WHAT ARE WE FACILITATING PEOPLE TO DO?

We are facilitating them to change! Small development activities can include but not be limited to sanitation and hygiene training, healthcare, literacy programs, training in nutrition and food production, skills training, and ethical and spiritual advisement. Whether the change is in a health practice, food production, educational system or even religion, we want to raise their awareness to problems in their midst and solutions within their grasp.

CHAPTER TEN: *BUT WHAT ABOUT ME?*

FUNDAMENTALS IN BRINGING CHANGE

Change will be a major issue confronting the poor. They will face shrinking assistance and resources.

Most aid programs basically have focused on people's economic needs believing that as long as people have enough money in their pockets they would be satisfied with their quality of life. This process is seen as a compassionate and generous since money or services are actually given to the recipients.

Until we catch the vision of focusing on the people's need to grow and develop according to aspirations chosen by them to control their own futures, we will continue to focus on their financial needs, while imposing decisions and expectations unto them, hindering their development.

If the poor are going to survive, we will need a whole new perspective on how to help the poor escape their poverty. The poor will need to do some changing. Change is necessary for survival.

BRINGING CHANGE IS A MATTER OF EXTREME CAUTION

Change is not always welcome. People can often undergo serious emotional struggles in facing change. Although one might consider change beneficial and in the best interests of the people, they might have different ideas as to what is best for them.

Despite the potential improvement in the change, some may prefer the old status for emotional reasons we may not discern.

Anger, loss of sentimental value, threat, loss of familiarity, loneliness, hopelessness, despair, feeling oppressed, loss of day-to-day routines, lack of control, insecurity, fear of the future, feelings of inferiority, low self-esteem, resentment, rights violated, fear of new technology are a whole check list of emotions that people go through in facing change.

We've all heard stories of the old widow who needs to be dragged out of her apartment in urban renewal situations. Even though planning for her future is secured, at least according to our plans, she may feel insecure with the threat of an unknown future and so will seek to avoid risks at all costs.

The dynamics of the emotional struggle people go through in facing change can be disturbing. To some, it implies loss where there is sadness or grief. To some it may come as a sacrifice at a cost that seems too great to bear. To many, the status quo is security and stability. How we handle these potential emotional responses is key. These responses ought not to be barriers if, indeed, the change is positive and welcomed by most of the people. *We need to help the people want change.*

Peter Batchelor in his book, *People in Rural Development,* relates the story of Mao-Tse Tung in China, when Mao recognized the importance of being slow to introduce new techniques to the people before they were ready for them. During the nineteen-sixties, he had a difference of opinion with senior agriculturalists in the government. The technocrats insisted that a break-through in food production would only be possible with a massive mechanization program. Mao insisted: "*The people must first be helped **'to want'** these changes.*"

As a result, a great effort was made to help the Chinese common people understand how political concepts, morale, and ethics relate to the struggle to work even harder, and be willing to try new techniques and equipment.

Only later was the push towards agricultural mechanization started. Mao was proved right: the technical advances in agriculture that took place after educating the people to the looming changes were a little short of miraculous. China now not only feeds her own massive population but also is a net exporter of rice and many other food products.

If change is to be enduring, we may need to deflect the prospect of the emotional turmoil people go through while leading them to the choice of "wanting" the change.[17]

HOPE FOR PERMANENT CHANGE CAN COME WHEN THE PEOPLE CAN BE LED THROUGH A SERIES OF SELF-EXAMINING QUESTIONS

The people must be led to decisions that can be embraced as their own in order for them to take ownership of the impending change. Taking ownership of what the people are expected to do is paramount in bringing about successful, permanent change in development. It is critical that the decisions be not imposed on them or performed through controlling or manipulating techniques. Facilitation by the community development worker is the process whereby people can arrive at decisions as if the solutions were discovered by themselves so that they feel they have done it by themselves.

17 Peter Batchelor, Rural Development, p.9

THE SERIES OF QUESTIONS BEGINS WITH:

"IS THIS CHANGE NECESSARY?" Will this change fill a need? The answer to this question will come from observations, research, and surveys, to determine whether what is being considered is truly necessary. Is it really a problem that needs improvement or is it just the "good idea" of an over-zealous development worker?

"IS THIS CHANGE DESIRED?" Have the people counted the cost? The second question will determine whether the change is something the people actually want. Do they really desire this change? Discussion and debate will occur in this stage as the people try to decide on pros and cons of the issue. It is not uncommon for people to decide that the change may be needed, but of low priority or simply that the timing of it is undesirable.

"IS THIS CHANGE POSSIBLE?" Is this change too far-fetched? The people need to appraise whether or not the change is within their limits and capabilities or is it beyond them, thus risking failure? Does the change require too great a leap for them in commitment and risk? This phase will ultimately evoke their decision.

"WHAT WILL THE PEOPLE DO?" This question is vital in ascertaining whether the people are eager to bring change. Without a firm agreement as to what the people will do for their part will make it risky to consider any undertaking. If this question is not satisfactorily answered, the development workers could end up doing it by themselves. To avoid moving into paternalism and dependency, to uncover any unintended imposed decisions, and to discern the firm intentions of the people to work toward the objective, this question must be clearly and decisively answered.

It is unwise to proceed with the people's development without these four questions being answered and the decisions faithfully carried out to a conclusion. The people must be prepared to take ownership in the area in which they are being engaged for change. There must be some investment of their own resources whatever they may be. Until these questions are answered one ought not to proceed.

PROVOKERS TO CHANGE –

The most effective time to bring change to a community is in a period of transition or when change is already happening. Sadly, often it is in a time of unfortunate circumstances such as in famine, health issues, refugee situations, migrations, loss of family, or even loss of financial security. People are most open when they are needy and perhaps under stress. In this type of transitional period people are more apt to listen to ideas since they are most vulnerable.

Unfortunately, it is in this period that they are prey to all sorts of evil schemes as well. It is not uncommon for widowed old ladies to be bilked out of their life savings on scams by people who appear to be genuinely concerned for their welfare. It may seem to Christians that it is a time of high vulnerability and therefore "unfair" even for Christians to intervene. But if Christians don't do it, we can be sure the evil doers will.

FUNDAMENTALS IN BRINGING CHANGE:

MOTIVATING FORCES –

As we discussed before, *Implementers* and *Followers* need motivating! The purpose is to stimulate an inward desire for some positive outcome. *Motivation* has as its objective the success and edification of those being motivated. As in sports, motivating the athletes is for their benefit as well as the coaches who are the motivators.

Motivation is stimulating people to make decisions and take actions over which they are going to feel good about themselves. Even in failure, if having been properly motivated, great consolation can come from one's having given it their best as reflected in their choices and actions.

The greatest motivating forces in the world are those rooted in love. The whole chapter in 1 COR:13 tells us that if any of our actions are based on something other than love, our intentions are suspect.

Manipulation, the counterfeit of motivation, is rooted in lust and has for its objective the gratification of the manipulator, often with little regard for those being manipulated.

The techniques of the manipulator are such that those being manipulated are moved in such a way as to be left not feeling good about themselves. They can feel tense and unsure and struggle with questions as to whether they've been used and abused. In the end, they will know that they've been manipulated.

MOTIVATION

MOTIVATION	VS.	MANIPULATION
- ROOTED IN LOVE		- ROOTED IN LUST
- FOR "YOUR" JOY		- FOR "MY" JOY
- GODLY STIMULI,		- UNGODLY STIMULI
- 2 COR 1:24		- THREATS, INTIMIDATION,
- BENEFITS, REWARDS		- BRIBES, COERCION
- PEOPLE FEEL GOOD ABOUT THEMSELVES		- PEOPLE DON'T FEEL GOOD ABOUT THEMSELVES
		- FEEL USED

Aware that the greatest motivating force in the world is rooted in love, how the outworking of that love is expressed in practical ways requires keen spiritual insight.

ROM 5:6-8 gives us clues as to perhaps the most powerful motivating force in the world.

"You see, at just the right time, when we were still powerless, Christ died for the ungodly. Very rarely will anyone die for a righteous man, though for good man someone might possibly dare to die. But God demonstrates His own love for us in this: While we were still sinners, Christ died for us." NIV

We may manifest great gifts of the spirit. We may have deep spiritual insight and can speak of matters great and lofty. We may speak in tongues, prophesy in power, heal the sick, and cast out demons because....*we believe in Jesus.*

But what these scripture verses tell us is that *Jesus believes in us.*

Jesus believes in us.

The passage says that we were powerless. We were heading toward zero quality of life. We were blinded, doing things over which we would be ashamed, all of them tending toward death, and...... just at the right time......*Jesus intervened.*

We had no hope, no options, no voice, and no prospects and yet he was ready and willing to lay down His life for us. Jesus came to our rescue. He didn't die for us because we were good; He died for us because we were no good.

He could have cast us off and thrown us on the garbage heap. He could have started with someone new, but He didn't, because He believed in us - that we could rise and believe. He cleaned us up, removed the rust, polished away the scratches and made us brand new. He believed in us and gave us another chance and still more chances. He never gave up on us, because He believed we were worth saving.

The greatest motivating force in the world is having someone believe in you. It spurs us to new hope and renewed effort. It is the great arouser, inspirer, and encourager. When someone believes in us we begin to believe in ourselves.

As Jesus believes in us, He wants us to go and believe in them - the downtrodden, disadvantaged, lost, and those without hope - that they can do it - that they can rise and believe and fulfill the destiny that God has for them. Believing in them is a powerful motivating force.

COMMON MOTIVATING FORCES:

1) BELIEVING IN THEM

What does "believing in them" actually mean? How is it worked out? We simply fall back on the "Pillars" for carrying out the practice of believing in them.

Image of God - we believe in them when we believe they have value, dignity , and worth.

The Body - we believe in them when we consider that they have a gifting, a competency that would allow them to make a fruitful contribution to the common good.

Acceptance - we believe in them when we can accept them for who they are, whatever their cultural heritage, customs and patterns and appreciate the differences between us.

Humility (Learner) - we believe in them when we demonstrate that we have something to learn from them and that we are somehow enriched by the relationship.

Servanthood - we believe in them when we want to see them successful in all that God has for them and are willing to work at it.

2) INFORMATION - is a powerful motivator. A good illustration is how advertising is such a potent stimulator for customers to make choices and take action. Advertising is simply information. Health, financial information, or statistics will attempt to get us to change our habits and behavior patterns. Whether it's a low fat diet, to quit smoking or refinance mortgages, behavior patterns of a whole nation can be changed as people count costs, weigh risks and seize opportunities just through information.

Use frequent repetition. Use as many media as possible. Appeal to as many senses as possible, hearing, seeing, putting a printout in their hands. Use lectures, slogans, posters, filmstrips, field trips, group discussion to disseminate information. Over-communicate. Repetition is a common need for those who struggle with literacy.

Awaretize with questions about inconsistencies and contradictions to help the people discover problems and solutions by themselves. Times will come when we can bring knowledge of opportunities within their reach as they identify their problems.

3) CLEAR-CUT TARGET (OBJECTIVE). -
PROV 29:18 - *"without a vision the people perish"* **KJV**
HAB 2:2 - *"write down the vision and make it plain, that others may run with it."* **KJV** I
COR 14:8 - *"...if the bugle's sound is uncertain, who will get ready for battle?"* ***NAB***

Nothing hinders change more than uncertainty. Make sure of your definitions , fine-tune your vision and objectives, and make your goals realistic and comprehendible. Articulate in such a way that the people clearly understand what it is they're being called to do. Write the vision down for the people to contemplate and avoid uncertainty as to what is implied and suggested.

4) REWARDS AND BENEFITS - A promised reward is a great motivator . When people can sense a tangible reward, they will be moved because there is something in it for them. A reward system is really biblical and not necessarily manipulative, as some people would suggest. The manipulator's method is to resort to bribe, threat, intimidation or even deception. Perverted behavior in no way edifies people or makes them feel good about themselves.

Someone might allege that by stressing rewards we make appeal to people's selfishness and greed. But all of God's promises in the Scriptures are based on incentives for obedience to His commands. For example, (paraphrasing) ***"if you believe in the Lord Jesus you will have everlasting life."*** The Lord's rewards are loving responses for our sacrificial effort to please Him. In many cases, the rewards can be for effort and motive alone rather than for accomplishment.

Development workers ought to define and articulate the rewards. For example, ***"if you boil your water, your children will not get sick!"*** The people should "want" to do what they're being encouraged to do because of the ultimate benefits. We ought to highlight the rewards with periodic reminders.

5) VOICE IN THE DECISIONS - It is amazing how people can be strongly motivated when they are given a say in the matter. When people are given a voice in the decisions they are stimulated since they have been allowed to contributeto the process. The whole process begins to be "theirs' as they take ownership of what is transpiring.

Having a voice is most helpful in identifying the problems of the community and having a voice toward solutions. The people become active participants when their input is valued and considered, even though their ideas are not necessarily adopted.

Conversely, if all decisions are handed down in a paternalistic fashion the people languish in passivity with low concern and participation. They become the objects (being done to) rather than the subjects (being the doer) of development.

6) COMMONLY FELT NEEDS - A commonly felt need in the community is a great motivator and unifier. Unity is built when the people face a common stress or threat, identify their problems collectively as a group, and take up a course of action.

7) CONTEXTUALIZE IT - Build on what they know. Find connection to something familiar and culturally relevant to their situation. Presenting ideas in connection with something they can identify with will give them more confidence and enthusiasm. Enthusiasm arouses interest. Building on what they know makes transitions easier and requires less training. It's essentially starting from a point at which they can have focus and not risk confusion or frustration.

8) MODELLING - Emphasize and show good examples. Define the actual goal in graphic terms. Show a working model, use videos, photos, and field trips. Visual demonstration is a great stimulus. It leaves less to misinterpretation. Seeing possibilities builds hopes and enthusiasm. Show them what a good job looks like whether you're building a wall or planting a garden.

9) ENABLEMENT - is investing the necessary training, tools and instructions in the people to get the job done. Grant the people what they need to be able to do the task. Enabling the people at the outset avoids inertia, delay, frustration, and confusion.

10) GET STARTED - Participation leads to more participation. The more participation the better since it creates a stimulus for the change to become permanent and self-sustaining. People will participate when they feel like the subjects and not the objects of the activity as they feel active and not passive.

"Give me some men who are stout-hearted men and I'll soon give you ten thousand more."

Lyrics from *The New Moon* by Sigmund Romberg,

Mr. Romberg understood something of human nature. When there are some who know they are valued, who will take up a worthy cause that will benefit many, there will be others to follow and join in the action. Participation breeds participation. Using our motivation protocols will be a great stimulus to participation.

PARTICIPATION IS VITAL:

- the people bring their unique giftings, skills, abilities, experience, and knowledge.
- people grow and develop by doing it in a group (community) and working together.
- by working together, the project has greater chance of becoming permanent.

<u>CHAPTER ELEVEN:</u> *BRING IT ON!*

<u>**HOW TO BRING CHANGE TO COMMUNITIES**</u> - There are two scripture passages that highlight principles on how to proceed in bringing change to communities.

<u>***SCRUTINIZE* YOUR FIELD**</u>

Expositors rarely stress the emphasis Jesus puts on the phrase

JOHN 4:35 " ***Behold, I say to you, lift up your eyes and look at the fields..."*** **NKJV-OB**

What Jesus is encouraging His disciples to do is a more intense action than simply seeing. They were *to consider, to contemplate*, at the same time they were looking. Paraphrasing, Jesus was saying, in effect, *scrutinize your field.* It was not to be just a cursory "look" but one that was deep and analytical. They were to look with a keen eye at all that they could observe. The community development practitioner ought to analyze the field of ministry in which God places them. They need to have a pulse on all that is going on socially, spiritually, intellectually and physically in that community.

<u>**PRACTICAL ADVICE**</u> **– 2 COR 10:13-16 (NKJV-OB)** - In these verses, Paul doesn't go into deep explanation as to the operative principles here, but defends his authority with a checklist of life principles and criteria under which he chose to labor in ministry. He defends his apostolate with the truth and power of these principles that authenticate and confirm his calling. We can glean practical hints to guide our own approach to ministry.

Paul asserts that he was to work ***"...but within the limits of the sphere which God has appointed us..."***

Paul gives what amounts to a workshop and the first precept he adopted in his approach to ministry was to stay within the limits of the sphere to which God had called him. God has appointed us *a sphere of ministry* in which we are to operate. We are to work within the limits of that sphere. It is there where we will have an "anointing" for effectiveness and results. That sphere will contain those to whom God has called us, ***"a sphere which especially includes you,"*** and expects no more from us than that. Beyond that sphere of operation lie overwork, stress, frustration, and perhaps even ineffectiveness.

Continuing in verse 14 Paul advocates discipline against over-extending ourselves:

"for we are not extending ourselves beyond our sphere - thus not reaching you, for it was to you that we came...."

We can infer from Paul that can we spread ourselves so thinly that we can jeopardize our effectiveness and miss the very people we are intended to reach. If we are not disciplined and constrained by our appointed mission we can become distracted, per-occupied and even overwhelmed by the needs around us, with the harmful results of.... ***"thus not reaching you."*** We are to keep our focus so that we fulfill the ministry to which God has called us.

In verse 15, Paul, upholding the vision, suggests that as he first ***"becomes enlarged"*** and effective with them, they can reach out together to the regions beyond them. First things first. *I will reach you and as you make greater progress and grow to maturity, we shall become "enlarged" together in experience to extend beyond our sphere.*

We ought to recognize that we cannot win the whole world by ourselves, nor does God intend that. We must be prepared to work within the limits of our sphere and let the Lord take care of the rest.

Knowing the ministry to which God calls us requires intercession, hearing the voice of God and planning! We need to hear from Him what He wants us to do. The principles of hearing God's voice and intercession are better discussed in Loren Cunningham's book, *Is That Really You God?*

Planning is clearly a godly principle. Winging it is not. Planning is not something that goes on because of a lack of confidence in the "word of the Lord," "going with the flow," or in "being led by the spirit." Planning and the " word of the Lord" are not mutually exclusive. Planning, guided by the Holy Spirit, with the principles of *scrutinizing our field* and realizing *the limits of our ministry* in mind, are foundational principles in the direction of our plan.[18]

Within the following framework, we will discern junctures at which we will need to seek God further as we proceed through our plan.

---

18 Loren Cunningham and Janice Rogers. Is That Really You, God? 2nd ed. (Hawaii : YWAM Publishing 2001)

1) ESTABLISH YOUR WORK AREA BASED ON:

A) SET BOUNDARIES - WHERE PEOPLE ARE CULTURALLY SIMILAR

It is a key factor in development to work with people who are similar in language, customs, habits, and even hopes and aspirations. A worker needs to seek every conceivable advantage for success in working with the poor. Avoiding potential troubling friction because of nationalistic, linguistic, religious or racial barriers may be necessary. Often it means setting actual geographical boundaries based on cultural populations wherein we ought to work.

Marie gave testimony of a coffee shop she had opened to minister to the prostitutes in King's Cross, a kind of central gathering area for wayward types in downtown Sydney, Australia. The original vision was to maintain a haven for the streetwalkers where they could come in for free coffee and doughnuts and receive respite from the action on the streets. The ministry was progressing nicely as the love, compassion and witness to the prostitutes began to touch their hearts. Several came to the Lord and, in fact, began to lead others to the Lord as well.

Almost imperceptibly, runaway teen-agers at King's Cross began to show up at the coffee shop, first in small, but then in greater numbers. Ministry to the teen-agers did not have quite the same success, as the teens were not usually there for respite as for the coffee and doughnuts and the convenience of a place to hang out. Imperceptibly as well, the prostitutes were coming in lesser numbers. Awareness of the problem had come too late to Marie, as she recognized that the prostitutes began not to come at all.

With the arrival of the teen-agers, the prostitutes felt that "their territory" was being invaded and intruded upon. They no longer felt that it was "their" coffee shop. In feeling their needs were no longer being met, they finally forsook the coffee shop and left it to the teen-agers.

It was heart breaking to hear Marie share her story in tears as she heard us share these principles. She knew without a doubt that she had been called to streetwalkers. Yet her unsuspecting, compassionate heart felt it was only natural to minister to the teen's needs as well, even though she felt no special calling to them. Because the groups were not separate according to their cultural similarity and identity, she eventually lost that streetwalker ministry to which God had called her and at which she was enjoying much success.

Q. WHAT COULD MARIE HAVE DONE TO RETAIN HER MINISTRY WITH THE STREET WALKERS?

B) WORK WHERE THERE IS THE ETHIC OF DEVELOPMENT IN THE PEOPLE

We have covered the drawbacks in working with people who have a low estimation of life and its prospects. It is not impossible but it can be time consuming, and discouraging in working with these types of people. It's almost as if they require a pre-development nurturing before they can be expected to contribute to a community process on their own. We must recognize this in communities as well as in individuals.

Overcoming their blame-shifting, low self-image and critical attitude toward life in general, would require a real reformation of their character and worldview. It can be done, but it is a slow, tedious process. To get them elevated to their true sense of worth, self-image, and attitude may require counseling and mentoring, rather than a development approach when they're not ready for it. The essential ingredient in working with the poor in development is whether or not they want to do something for themselves. People without the development ethic are not yet primed to do that. Look for people with a development ethic.

ETHIC OF:

DEVELOPMENT	UNDERDEVELOPMENT
DO THEY SEE THEMSELVES AS ABLE?	SEE THEMSELVES AS INADEQUATE?
BELIEVE THEY CAN BRING CHANGE?	ARE THEY FATALISTIC?
SEE "NEW" WEALTH AS POSSIBLE?	WANT REDISTRIBUTION?
CAN THEY START SMALL?	FEEL OWED? SEE THEMSELVES AS VICTIMS?
DO THEY VALUE TIME?	REGARD TIME CASUALLY?
DO THEY LOOK FOR OPPORTUNITIES?	ARE THEY APATHETIC?
DO THEY SHUN DEPENDENCY?	INDIFFERENT TO DEPENDENCY?
DO THEY HONOR SUCCESS &	ARE THEY CRITICAL OF SUCCESS?
HONOR INDIVIDUAL CREATIVITY?	EXPECT CONFORMITY?
IS THERE EQUALITY OF PERSONS?	IS THERE INEQUALITY OF PERSONS?
DO THEY BELIEVE IN MAN'S DOMINION?	SEE NATURE AS UNCONTROLLABLE?
ACCEPT DIVERSITY?	DO THEY EXPECT UNIFORMITY?
ARE MORAL QUESTIONS CONFRONTED?	IS CORRUPTION A ROUTINE WAY OF LIFE ?
IS WORK VALUED?	IS WORK VIEWED AS A CURSE?
LOOK FOR IMPROVEMENT?	ARE THEY PESSIMISTIC?
SEEK FUTURE POSSIBILITIES?	DO THEY FEAR FAILURE?
SEIZE RESPONSIBILITY?	AVOID RESPONSIBILITY?
ACCEPT CONSEQUENCES?	DO THEY BLAME SHIFT?
SPEAK LIFE INTO COMMUNITY?	SPEAK DEATH INTO COMMUNITY?

FOR DISCUSSION: HOW TO EVALUATE A COMMUNITY'S POTENTIAL?

C) WHERE POPULATION IS A MANAGEABLE NUMBER

"Those who would change the world began by doing it locally, in clusters of like-minded people, with a single ideological purpose." John Naisbitt in *Megatrends*

We are not expected to do all the Lord's work by ourselves, nor all at once.

The precept of working within the limits of our sphere implies that we ought to work with an amount of people that is a manageable number. This number would be the community with which we can interact on some regular basis. We need to know the people and they need the opportunity to know us. If we are dealing with a population number that is so unwieldy that we cannot become familiar with the people, their habits, and customs, we will lose the opportunity to build trust and risk not gaining the participation of the people.

A team of eight workers in the Tondo squatter zone of Manila which has a population of over fifteen thousand people would have greater potential for success by selecting a smaller zone of population where the people have a development ethic. Basically, in their planning, the team would line off a zone with geographical boundaries within which they will work, thereby limiting the amount of people to a more workable, reasonable number and concentrate their focus on that area.

The same holds true for a small team working among the million Muslims in their quadrant of the city of New Delhi. Once it was decided that the Muslim quadrant could actually be demarcated according to national identity sectors such as the Iraqis, Iranians, Saudis, Afghanis, etc. the team could identify and begin with a more manageable number and keep their outreach limited to those who were of the same national origin and culturally similar. The Iranians and Iraqis, for example, do not get along, so for expediency sake, ministry to those groups should be conducted separately. This would follow the principles of working with people who are actually culturally similar and yet reduced to a more manageable number.

I've been challenged by students in advocating these precepts, since it seems insensitive to help people on the one hand, while at the same time excluding those who might be in close proximity to the original group with which you're working. That criticism might seem valid if our intention is to bring about development all by ourselves. On the other hand, if we put development in the hands of the people, we will realize the most rapid multiplication of improvements will spread from people to people faster than if we try and do it all by ourselves. If the innovation is worthwhile, it will multiply and spread on its own merit to the other postponed areas. We're not excluding the other areas only postponing them. Ideally, we want the knowledge of the innovation to spread like wildfire. That will only happen if the people are encouraged and motivated to pass on to others what they have learned. As they freely receive, they should be encouraged to freely give and pass it on. It's part of a discipling process even for unbelievers. For example, it's been Frank Laubach's[19] *great idea that those who are being taught to read, ought to teach others as they themselves are being taught. That enhances multiplication. That's the great concept for spreading the Gospel and multiplying churches.*

19 Frank Laubach (1884-1970) founder of Laubach Literacy. Developed the "Each One Teach One" literacy program to teach people to read in their own language.

For our purposes here, it's good to set boundaries where people are culturally similar and work with a manageable number of people who have a development ethic.

D) WHERE SERVICES AND SUPPLIES ARE AVAILABLE LOCALLY

Avoid using outside resources where possible. We're not suggesting that communities should reinvent the wheel but rather avoid the pitfall of becoming dependent. If supplies and resources are not available locally, there is no risk of dependency when the people have paid from their means to obtain them.

It was interesting listening in on a meeting of local, island supervisors of the Department of Transportation on Guam, in the West Pacific, discussing plans for a new up-to-date map of the island. Their plan was to have a functional as well as commercially appealing map/brochure to promote tourism interests to the island.

Following a discussion of ideas with no solution looming and a resulting stalemate, one supervisor suggested they should hire consultants from Los Angeles on the mainland U.S. to help get the job done. The chairman superintendent, while attempting to control his temper, waved his index finger around the meeting table at the other members and said in somber tones that they did not have to look to experts in Los Angeles, because there was enough ability and brainpower right there at the table.

He was not going to consult outside sources but challenged their thinking to get on with ideas of their own. Needless to say, they eventually came up with a very colorful, attractive, accurate, and functional map, one in which they took enormous island pride and satisfaction. They did it themselves. It was a huge leap and success for their development.

E) ONE SHOULD BEGIN WORK WHERE THE NEEDS INTERSECT WITH A PROBABILITY OF SUCCESS.

Start with an area where the potential looks bright for success. If the needs are great or overwhelming, perhaps what is needed is relief rather than development. We do not want to risk failure or have the people become discouraged and reinforce feelings of inadequacy that they can't do it. There should be some probability of success.

Several people have chided me with comments that we advocate working only with situations so controlled and of such ideal conditions as to be risk-free. If we reflect on our true objectives and remember what it is that should concern us; we'll realize that we want every conceivable prospect for success for ***the people's sake*** *and not our own.* *It's not our resume that needs enhancing or our personal satisfaction.*

We're not trying to build our reputation on grand schemes and accomplishments, we're trying to help the people grow and develop. We want to give them every advantage for success that will build their self-confidence and enhance their self-image, surely, at least, in the beginning.

We're not looking for projects that have no obvious value, as the people will sense the hollowness of the effort and achievement. We do want to address felt needs. The principle is still the same. We want try something that's within their grasp with the probability of a quick success. All this must be covered by intercession and hearing the voice of God.

BRINGING CHANGE TO COMMUNITIES CONT'D.

2) WORK WITHIN THE STRUCTURE - Many cases of failure in development work have come because workers felt compelled to work outside the authority structures in communities, instead of within them. Often, we've thought that we needed to do our work despite them. In some more extreme and bizarre cases, development agencies have felt the temptation to seek justification to ignore them.

It is not within our purpose to discuss the elements that advocate the neutralizing of existing community structures that appear to hinder the people's growth and development. We advocate working within the structure. If that becomes impossible, we advocate moving on to some other community.

Often, it's difficult to understand the resistance of those in authority to development, but we ought to make a self-examination first to make sure we're not at fault. Unless the hearts of those in authority are transformed, we'll likely face their opposition though we may never know why. What may be required is a real reformation of their character as through a conversion transformation. Needless to say, we are not ignorant to the injustices and oppression that go on around the world driven by land monopolies, exorbitant interest rates, dishonest landlords, corrupt magistrates, police, and politicians. It is a fact of life that these situations exist. Until those in authority and their constituencies cultivate a community and social responsibility, our prospects of working within the group are minimized.

Many in authority, however, actually do have the welfare of their people in mind. The classic illustration of working within the structure is illustrated in *Bruchko* the exciting book by Bruce Olson. The hill tribe Motilone Indians were being threatened with an epidemic of conjunctivitis (pink eye). If not treated properly and quickly, it could result in serious or permanent eye damage or even blindness.

An element of "structure" in that tribe of Indians was their witch doctor who was treating the eye infections with herbs, potions, incantations, and concoctions of various types. The only thing that would heal those infections was treatment with an antibiotic eye salve that Bruce had in his supplies.[20]

Bruce could easily have stepped to the forefront in that community to cure the infections like some hero and win the personal esteem and gratitude of the whole tribe. Instead, he strongly tried to convince the witch doctor to treat the eye infections of the villagers with the antibiotic eye salve. He went so far as to cause the infection by rubbing the pus from one of the villagers in his own eyes to persuade the witch doctor of the effectiveness and security of his treatment. When she saw the results and effectiveness of the salve on Bruce's infection, she was convinced to use it on the rest of the tribe and the epidemic was thwarted.

As a result of working within the structure, instead of Bruce becoming the rescuer of the people, the witch doctor's reputation was maintained. By working within the structure, Bruce did not diminish the standing of the witch doctor in the eyes of the villagers but made of her a friend. The witch doctor thus became more open to new and different innovations suggested by Bruce. Instead of making a rival or a competitor of the witch doctor, Bruce had won an ally who became a channel for Bruce's future initiatives with the Motilones, their eventual conversion, and wide-ranging development. Significant too, was the fact that Bruce allowed this process to take hold in the community without making the people dependent on himself. Working within the structure will bring lasting results through the buildup of trust in the worker.

3) LOOK FOR SMALL BEGINNINGS

I COR 1:26-28 - the world chooses the attractive, strong, rich and clever.
GOD - chooses the afflicted, poor, weak and foolish
ZECH 4:10 - consoling, comforting, instructional?

ZECHARIAH 4:10 - has often been used by sincere Christians as a kind of a consolation verse to bring comfort when feeling the pains of fruitless and seemingly ineffective ministry. We languish that we may not have had the desired results to our work. We rationalize that even though we may not have had fruitful ministry, at least we "planted some seeds." Then, too, "doesn't the Lord say don't despise the days of small beginnings." Hence, the verse is used to bring us comfort and consolation.

20 Bruce E. Olson, *Bruchko* p. 129-136

I believe there is more to this verse than just comfort and consolation. I believe this verse is instructional. The Lord is saying; in essence, don't turn your nose up at a small beginning. Look for small beginnings. He said to Bethlehem Ephrata,

MICAH 5:2 "...*though you are little among the thousands of Judah, yet out of you shall come forth to me the one to be ruler in Israel...*," **NKJV-OB**

The Lord told Gideon for almost any excuse to send more than 99% of his army home. God said that with less than 1% of your recruits, you will conquer , so that you and your men would know that I'm the One bringing the victory. God wants us to be on the lookout for small beginnings.

While on Guam, I attended monthly association meetings of the various ministers and missionaries on the island. At one such meeting, an elderly pastor announced that the local Guamanian hospital was very short on help. The suggestion was for all the ministers to announce to their congregations the critical need for volunteers at the hospital. I suggested to my wife Ursula, to go to the hospital and enquire as to how our little mission team could be of service. I made the suggestion since I thought it was a timely opportunity for us to do our little part in support of the local community.

Ursula started going to the hospital one morning a week for about 2 hours each time to feed infirmed and senile patients. That expanded to two mornings a week and eventually with another team member accompanying Ursula for the two mornings a week for two hours each time. The patients were not truly ill but invalid. They were unable to wash, groom or feed themselves without considerable effort.

One morning, a newspaper reporter was walking through the ward and was surprised to see the two women of our team doing such unattractive, volunteer work. After a brief conversation, he decided to write a story about them and their volunteer work, which was published in the newspaper complete with photo and all.It was a stroke of favorable coverage for our small team that labored under a lukewarm acceptance by local evangelical churches as well as some of the main-line traditions.

It seems the newspaper had many curious readers enquire as to the nature of our organization and why it was that we were volunteering while their own people were not. In any case, for whatever reason, the newspaper decided to do a follow-up feature story on Ursula, myself, and the organization we represented. The story, with photos, covered at least a half newspaper page.

Not to be outdone, the one, local television station on Guam decided to run a promotion to select the person who made the greatest contribution to community life on the island for that year. They selected Ursula as that person and interviewed her on television for the broadcast of their Christmas community program. Ursula was interviewed in living color, giving testimony to the Lord Jesus and the love that He had for those elderly and debilitated people. It was not a brief interview by most television standards, but a full-on testimony for the Lord. All that came about because one person offered to do a small part to serve the local community.

The story did not end there. Next to the hospital where Ursula volunteered was the office of a government agency that taught skills training to adults with learning disability. If you're unacquainted with adults with learning disability and their condition, perhaps you can imagine a child that has grown to be about 25-30 years old who is unable to hold normal conversations, feed themselves properly, shave themselves, or exercise the smallest of skills. The female director of that agency, on reading of our story in the newspaper, called us and asked if we could do some volunteer work at her agency, as well.

Ursula and Marlene, in addition to their time at the hospital, then went to the agency next door to help with the adults with learning disability. I personally went with them one afternoon a week, to help with the special case of a young man who was bound up as a mute in his hearing, seeing, and speaking. Often, he would have violent fits of temper.

At the outset, we did not know that the director of that agency requesting our help was the wife of a Guamanian Senator of the territory legislature. Through our volunteering at her agency and our mutual faith in Jesus, we became friends.

When a special election was called to replace the incumbent governor of Guam, it turned out that the Senator-husband of our agency friend became the new governor. We then were friends with the First Lady of Guam who facilitated us in every facet of our ministry.

All this from a small beginning

****

Past failures have come from trying to teach people too much. The poor usually cannot cope with complexity. Give the people a chance to be faithful in little things. We want to start small because large plans are too complex - too slow to achieve. People can become discouraged and convinced they can 't do it. We want to start small because we want a *quick success* - a winnable victory.

A quick success builds enthusiasm and participation and gets the people believing in themselves. It builds trust in the worker.

Usually the poor lack experience, organization, and confidence. We want to present challenges within their grasp, something with which they're familiar and builds on what they know.

- something simple, low risk,
- because multiplication throughout the community is easier
- teaching innovations is easier when not too complex
- having them teach others is easier

In smaller projects, it's easier to observe potential leaders and the community minded individuals.

We will encourage the following two principles to be used in tandem.

4) USE A SEQUENCE OF CHANGES - At the outset we want avoid undertaking programs and refrain from a range of simultaneous activities. Keep the vision simple - first one change, then a second, then a third rather than having two or more changes going on at the same time. Allow the people to focus on singular, small changes to build their confidence. In tandem, with the principle of undertaking the primary change (#4) also use the principle of pursuing one-step at a time (#5) in that change.

5) STEP BY STEP – ISAIAH 28:9-10 - *"Whom will he teach knowledge? And whom will he make to understand the message? Those just weaned from the milk? Those just drawn from the breasts? For precept must be upon precept, precept upon precept, line upon line, line upon line, here a little, there a little."*

NKJV-OB

Isaiah asks the questions of whom do you want to teach and whether you want them to understand your message? He suggests that we ought to consider them as newborn babes just weaned from the breasts and still on milk - not yet ready for solid food. The process is to lead them through a simple approach of one undertaking at a time in a step-by-step advance with only a little at a time.

Keeping the process simple will have greater potential for being understood and apprehended by the people.

When our daughter was trying to teach our young grandson the names of colors she kept teaching him and then quizzing him on a variety of different objects of various colors. Our grandson was having limited to poor success. When I suggested that she pick various objects all of the same color and then repeat the same color no matter what the object was, he began to grasp his colors quickly. This was possible as he simply learned one color at time.

MATT 25:21 - suggests that success will most likely follow small, concerted efforts handled faithfully, legitimizing an expansion then to greater and loftier things.

THE FOLLOWING IS A SCHEMATIC ILLUSTRATING THE PROCESS OF INITIATING CHANGE.

Let's suppose three areas of need have been identified in the community: food production (or AGR for agriculture) literacy (LIT) and a health clinic (HLT).

After consideration and deliberation, it was decided by the community to initiate a change at this time only in food production (AGR) while foregoing any attempt at literacy or health. They would be following the principle of using a sequence of changes.

First, it was to be agriculture.

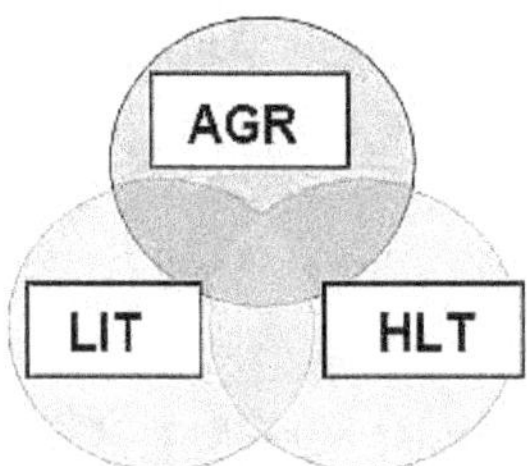

Within agriculture as our beginning, we initiate training and instruction with only one topic at a time that's relevant to agriculture in a step by step process.

We may want to start with seeds and instruction in storage, keeping them dry and free from vermin and so on. Then we go onto training in soil management regarding top soil, erosion prevention, clearing from rocks and stones and so on. Then we go on to fertilizers and irrigation and so on until we've covered all relevant instruction to Agriculture in the step-by-step process.

ETC.
HARVESTING
IRRIGATION
FERTILIZER
SOIL
SEEDS

If all other considerations are in place, we are now prepared to undergo our process of bringing change to increase our harvest and food production.

Following the success of the Agriculture program, we then can go on to the Literacy program or Health clinic according to our choice using the same process of sequence of change in a step-by-step format.

6) MODELLING - MODEL! MODEL! MODEL! We can never mention enough the role modeling can play in development efforts from the standpoint of inspiring and motivating the people. Always show them what a working model looks like. Use films, field trips, whatever. Help them envision the future outcome of their efforts. Recall, too, the method of passing on your skills of I do - you watch/, we do - we watch/, you do - I watch.

7) PHASE-OUT - Wisdom dictates that you give periodic reminders that an end is coming and that the people, at some point, will have to take over. Jesus did that with his disciples. He said that where He was going they could not follow. Phasing yourself out with reminders serves as an incentive to the people that if they want development to happen they need to become earnest in implementing change. It communicates to the people that you believe in them and that you have confidence in their ability to take over and bring success to their efforts.

DEVELOPMENT A MATTER OF THE HEART [21]

by Fred Gregory

World Concern/Adam Buchanan

When I first met the people in Bajua, Bangladesh, they were destitute and barely surviving. Many had been refugees in India during the Bangladesh War of Liberation. The war had destroyed everything they owned except what they could carry.

They had come to the point of pleading for help – food, clothing and shelter. Children and adults were dying of malnutrition and disease; women could not come out in public because their clothes were so tattered that they were not adequately covered; most children had no clothes; many of the men had gone away to the city to find employment as laborers.

Today, the rice paddy fields are harvested by men and women two or three times a year. Tidy clusters of houses form villages where the people happily engage in healthy village life. People are not dying because of lack of food. Children are going to school. Dignity is seen in the faces of the people of Bajua again. They talk about what they are going to do in the future.

A partnership was developed between caring Christians in North America and the people of Bajua. This relationship enabled the people of Bajua to engage in a development process which moved them from a life of destitution to one of dignity. Self-worth was restored and they took control of their lives in positive ways. That is what development is all about.

WHAT ARE THE RESULTS OF DEVELOPMENT?

My friends in Bajua, Bangladesh, provide us with a wonderful example of what happens when people have the opportunity to develop. There are many results of development. We will focus on three.

1. Development reduces the need for relief

Since those first desperate days when they returned from India as refugees, the people of Bajua have needed very little outside relief assistance. They now grow all the food they need. Many sell their excess rice, which provides cash for building better houses. They have money to pay for medical treatment and medicines. Their children go to school. They have money to buy improved seed varieties and tools. They are adequately clothed.

Because people have built better houses, annual windstorms do not cause as much damage as before. Because people are healthier, they are less vulnerable to disease and epidemics. Cropping patterns have been diversified to reduce the risks of growing only one crop. Because they now have savings in their cooperative groups, they have access to cash for emergencies.

Cyclones and floods are still an annual reality in Bangladesh. The effects, however, of these natural phenomena are not nearly as great as they once were for the people of Bajua. The winds still blow as hard as ever, but now the people are better prepared and can recover, using their own resources.

2. Development enables people to use their own resources

One of the myths of poverty is that poor people, especially poor people in the undeveloped world, have no resources. The people of Bajua taught me that there are many resources available which are often overlooked by those of us trying to help.

I learned that there is an abundance of creativity and energy when people see themselves as successful.

After the first crop was harvested, and farmers had received their cash for the crop and saved seed for the next crop, they immediately began to think of new and creative ways to earn even more money.

Before, they had paid local money lenders 200-350 percent interest on the money they borrowed to plant their crops. Now, with small grants from the North American partner agency, each cooperative administered small loans to

21 Fred Gregory, *Development a Matter of the Heart* (Seattle, Washington: World Concern 1981) Reprinted by permission21

Fred Gregory began his career in international relief and development in 1966, working with war victims in Vietnam. He went to Bangladesh to initiate rehabilitation and development projects following that country's War of Independence in 1972. Fred serves as World Concern's Director of International Programs.

farmers who paid 10 percent interest. Because the system was just, farmers saw a direct correlation between their hard work and income. They immediately began thinking of ways to further cut expenses, because that meant more return on their investment of cash and labor.

Because the War of Independence had taken so many lives, there were many old people without adult children to care for them. A program was initiated whereby the elderly who had no family were "adopted" by other families. This once again gave meaning and purpose to people who had lost their reason for living. They were given productive tasks, and again felt like a useful part of the village.

Many women had lost their husbands in the war as well. Normally, widows were at the mercy of the community for their survival. At the urging of the Bengali project director, land was set aside for women to farm, and a women's cooperative was started. Since farming was traditionally only men's work, this was a very risky idea. In the end, all the cooperatives agreed to the idea. Within the first year, the women's groups had better yields than the men's cooperatives. Instead of wanting small diesel rotivator tractors, they were demanding Massey-Ferguson tractors! While that wasn't necessarily a good idea for that time and place, they at least were thinking big, and about possibilities they had never dreamed of before.

A fishing cooperative was organized for landless people. That grew from a few small boats and fishing nets into a cooperative of over 400 families, each with a boat. They created marketing systems to sell their catch. Today their fishing industry is thriving.

Another cooperative was formed for women to chop wood to sell in the city for fuel wood. Cooperative-owned boats brought logs from government approved cutting areas to their work area. The boats then took the chopped firewood to the city to be sold at the maximum price, cutting out middlemen at each step.

Creativity and energy were in abundance when the rewards for labor were fair and just.

3. Development allows people to have more control over their lives

For years, villagers in Bajua had wanted schools for their children. The government had not established schools in many isolated rural areas. Several villages decided that they would start their own schools and pay for them through cooperative dues. People who had a fourth- or fifth-grade education were hired to teach the children. The villagers built bamboo and thatch shelters which became schools. The children learned to write with reed pens, using charcoal ink, writing on leaves. These schools were the pride of the communities.

Health is always important to people. Instead of an outside agency (or the government) starting a health program, the cooperatives charged their members fees and started their own prepaid health plan. They hired a practical nurse who provided health services. Later, a doctor was hired who took referrals from the village nurses. This effort became an example of what could be done by people working together.

With the establishment of a more secure economic system, people took control of their children's education and village health care needs.

Previously poor farmers began running for village and county political office. With the first election, 100 percent of the cooperative members who ran for office were elected. Historically, only wealthy land-owners and businessmen were ever elected to office. Farmers began to take control of their families and communities because they now had hope in the future and in each other.

With more cash being generated in these rural cooperatives, the banks began to see an advantage in having branch offices in this remote place. Today, these once destitute people have access to banking services never before available to them.

A Matter of the Heart

Development is really a matter of the heart, and not simply of projects which are often described in development terms. The critical factors are internal, not external.

By the reestablishment of self-worth and dignity, the people of Bajua were able to have hope for a better future, and they acted on that hope.

World Concern believes that helping people help themselves is the key to ending the cycle of poverty. Our field-workers use their professional skills to assist people and communities in their quest for self-sufficiency and control over their lives. This process of working together usually needs to include four simple ingredients. They are:

1. People must want the problem solved. This instills ownership of the idea in people's minds.
2. The solution must be in their means to achieve – it is possible to do.
3. People must have faith in each other. Trust relationships are essential.
4. Activities must start with the simple problems and move to the more complex.

World Concern recognizes that people must be dealt with as whole persons, with a wide variety of needs which are inter-linked. To meet these inter-linked needs, we have developed technical expertise in food production, animal husbandry, health care, water development and leadership training. These areas of expertise open doors of opportunity to minister in many other ways as well.

We all have physical, emotional, social and spiritual needs which must be met. Engaging in the development process in a healthy way means we all must learn from each other. Professional experts must learn from those they serve. Those whom we serve must understand that they have value and much to teach us as well. When that exchange can happen, development can take place in all of our lives. WC

Mr. Gregory, currently the assistant to the President of George Fox University, recently reported that although this article was written in 1981, this program still operates in S Bangladesh and is self-sustaining. It is called CSS/Christian Service Society and is completely governed and run by Bangladeshis.

CHAPTER TWELVE: *WHAT'S OUR GAME PLAN?*

Among the sad discouragements one can experience in reviewing one's work is to conclude that it was ineffective or wasted because of a perceived lack of positive results. We can be troubled over what may be regarded as a low return on our investment of time and effort.

Realizing early that there were guideposts along the way, which might have signaled a need for adjustments to our work, could have avoided meager outcomes. Missionaries coming off the field after years of trying to alleviate poverty conditions have come back admitting that, despite their efforts, the poor have remained largely poor and their work unrewarding for lack of fruit. Nowhere has this been more prevalent than in ministries that seek to elevate the poor through development work.

In our earlier discussion on the skills of a facilitator, we'll recall that one skill that was important was that of being an evaluator. It's useful in all work to exercise that skill by monitoring, listening, appraising, seeking feedback, and constantly being attentive to the progress of our project.

It is easier to make adjustments midstream while the project is under way, rather than wait until the end to make corrections or modifications. Adjustments at the end might be so serious as to require the whole project to be done over. Doing the job over again can be exasperating and can cause a loss of confidence in leaders and development workers. A good facilitator/evaluator will monitor progress intermittently in relaxed fashion, without appearing to be a watchdog or jail house warden. While monitoring progress, it is also timely to compliment on the good job underway.

The signals that we ought to look for to indicate we're on track in development work are generated within the people themselves. If we look only to the progress of the project itself, we could be making a fundamental error. These signals can be discerned in what we might call the:

***RESPONSES OF THE PEOPLE*.**

In our efforts, if we do not see these tendencies being expressed by the people, we need to make adjustments until we do see them. We will need to analyze what the problem is and step back until we see the necessary responses developing in the people. The first response we need to sense within the people is...

a) TRUST.- Poor and needy people of disadvantaged communities can be genuinely accommodating and deferring but we may not necessarily have their trust. Building trust is the foundation of all relationships but particularly with those on whom life has placed a heavy burden. If we are expecting to mobilize a people even when it's to their benefit, gaining their trust is our responsibility. Being the outsider, it's up to us.

Trust can be enhanced by the workers willingness to adapt to the culture, learn their language, and adapt overall to the lifestyle of the people with which they're working.

A willingness to be vulnerable in relationships quickly communicates a readiness to receive other people's ideas and opinions. Two-way relationships encourage trust. A one-way attitude wherein the facilitator is the only source of ideas incites reserve in the people which is hurtful since their participation and cooperation are needed. Generally, as the C.D. workers listen to their ideas, the people are ready to accept ideas from them.

Doing physical work, getting our hands dirty with them, solving problems together will accelerate trust. There is a bonding that comes through working with the people. If we want to avoid being treated like a guest which hinders closeness and intimacy, we need to find ways to work with the people.

Trust will grow as we *communicate contextually*. If they like story telling than that's an appropriate communication device we need to learn. We may need to become adept at using metaphors and comparisons that are relevant to the culture in which we work.

Being a worker who *builds on what they know* will bring endearment and trust quickly. We can discourage people by trying to take them too fast too soon or by having unrealistic expectations.

Trust will come when we exhibit a disposition to hinder dependency. The people will perceive your intentions to act only as a facilitator and they will trust you for it. People will discern if you are out to control them and may quickly draw back.

As C.D. workers display an attitude of the *"Pillars"* and those concepts are operational in their lives the people will easily display trust. If the C.D. workers see them as having dignity and worth, with abilities to help the group, accept them as they are, concede that they have something to learn from the people, and are not there to dominate but to see the people successful, the people will not only trust the workers, but will love them.

b) PARTICIPATION - When we have the trust of the people, the next expected response we need from them is their *participation*. We must have their participation if development work is to succeed and endure. Otherwise, they will not take ownership of the project. The great qualifier in stimulating participation is that they become the active and not passive participants in the development process. They must become involved rather than just spectators allowing the imposition of outside programs or agendas to control their destiny. As they become the subjects, they become the implementers and beneficiaries of the development process. We facilitate them in the change process.

Inherent in stimulating as much participation as possible has got to be our confidence in The Body principle. We need as much participation as possible to achieve inclusion of as many skills, gifts, experiences and competencies as possible. The greater the number of participants, the greater potential for inclusion of all the needed skills to achieve the objective within the people's resources, and for reducing the risk of dependency on outside sources. Community development in action is trusting that everyone has some contribution to make to the welfare and progress of the group.

As we trust in this principle and encourage people to exercise their abilities, we will see a growing tendency in them to explore and risk their own creativity, with decreasing timidity in sharing their ideas. That increases feelings of self-worth which leads to increasing confidence. As they become more confident, they will seek increasing control of the decisions which affect them and be on the road to development.

If we are experiencing little or no participation, we may be failing in proper motivation technique. If the people are not joining in, it may be something in our manner or process that may be hindering trust. We may need to go over the several principles of building trust to evaluate our methods.

c) PLANNING - When people are showing up, taking interest in discussions, and are demonstrating tendencies to get involved, the stage is being set for growth toward the next level of development which is planning.

The Bible has a lot to say about planning.

PROV 21:5 - "The plans of the diligent lead surely to plenty, but those of everyone who is hasty surely to poverty." **NKJV-OB**

The Bible's characterization of someone without a plan is one who is hasty. The next progressive response in a people's development has to do with their willingness to plan.

For many poor people, while living practically hand to mouth and on the brink of elimination, planning for them seems to be futile. In their pressures, they don't seem to have enough resources in hand, long enough, even to imagine going about a process that requires an outlook to the future. The pressure for them is just to make it through another day. Simply put, planning for the poor is a process of utilizing their resources in the most effective way because needs are great, and resources are few.

The beauty of planning is that it is not only a way out of a struggling situation, but that it challenges their outlook to think futuristically. Planning confronts their get-through-the-day mentality by compelling them to invest work and resources for some future pay-off. It also encourages *goal setting* for them. They begin to focus on possible targets for them and their children.

We should never underestimate this undercurrent of hope lurking in the hearts of poor people for their children. It can be a powerful force. They simply may want their children to learn to read, grow up without a host of sicknesses, or have gainful employment. Goals can be simple and fundamental in the beginning and as confidence rises, aspirations rise and so will goals.

Planning will stimulate *budgeting* which becomes a discipline to give structure to development. Budgeting will give them insight into their resources and inventories on what is discretionary and how much are fixed. As they exercise choices in allocating finances and resources, that nurtures discipline and stewardship at the same time.

As *planning, goal setting, and budgeting* become positive activities, so will their development of simple administrative skills. As the people undertake record keeping habits such as saving payment receipts, calculating projected expenses, and tabulating sources of income, they will be acquiring small, administrative skills that move them along in their development.

The whole notion of planning within the community combats the spirit of fatalism, the ethic of underdevelopment, and the culture of poverty syndrome as the people begin a work-for-the-future ethic. By investing in the future, people begin raising their hopes and expectations and they begin an ascent on a development spiral.

d) DECISION - MAKING - The natural outgrowth of planning and its added processes of goal setting, budgeting and administration is *decision-making*.

To this point, in our ***Responses of the People***, we have seen a kind of pre-development that might be characterized as preparation. The next logical step in their sequential growth, wherein they actually begin to take ownership of what they are expected to do, is *decision-making*.

Making decisions will challenge them as they realize the care and stewardship that need to be exercised. A strong stimulus to their growth will be the challenge of orienting their sense of *priorities* through making difficult and sometimes painful decisions. As we choose options based on our hopes and aspirations with established criteria, we move toward growth and maturity. Decision-making becomes a time of stretching confidence, level of commitment and the depth of determination. It is the great foster-parent to ownership. If the people have input and a voice in decisions, they will likely flow with the action, as they feel a part of them has invested in the process. Taking ownership reinforces the sense that the process is really theirs and will motivate them to work toward its ultimate success.

e) RESPONSIBILITY - The next level in the upward progress of a people's development is *responsibility.* (A tendency in people to take control of decisions is healthy to a point. Anyone can make decisions.)Most of us would have no problem in being the one who exercises authority. Simply pushing the buttons to have the rest of the people take action is easy. The challenge is whether we are willing to follow through to completion. If at the first sign of trouble, we look to give up on our plans we will not convey a sense of stability . In leaders, it does not instill confidence in one's followers. What gives our decision-making legitimacy is our mental toughness and willingness to take the responsibility for the decisions we make. Pursuing one's choices to completion despite setbacks, mistakes, or sometimes opposition is a sign of stability, reliability and maturity.

f) ACCOUNTABILITY - The last and most encouraging of these growth responses in the people is their willingness to live with the consequences of their choices. When they are mentally strong enough to risk making decisions, willing to pursue those choices to completion, and accept the consequences whatever the outcome, we can confidently believe the people are on the road to development and that they are "good risks." Despite possible failures, they can be deemed worthy of other future attempts.

CHAPTER THIRTEEN: *GOING FOR IT!*

SCHEMATIC SUMMARY OF PROCESS IN COMMUNITY DEVELOPMENT

As facilitators in the development process our activity begins with the ***EXPLORATORY*** phase. During this phase, we are living among the people and building a base of information. We are acquiring knowledge of their customs, culture, and behavior patterns. Ideally, we are trying to identify with the people and experience life with them. We are observing and noting their levels of development using LUKE 2:52 as our guide.

As our necessary relationships develop in the community, we may begin the process of lifting people's awareness to inconsistencies, stimulating them to recognize and identify problems and whether changes might be helpful.

It is in this opening ***EXPLORATORY PHASE*** that we try to answer the major question of whether a change is necessary.

EXPLORATORY

INFO-GATHERING/BRINGING

AWARETIZATION

IS THIS CHANGE NECESSARY??

Next, in *the* ***INTEGRATION PHASE***, with some of their problems identified, we would introduce discussion about opportunities within the people's reach.

In this phase, they are moved to consider the possibilities of change by going through a period of reflection. Discussions within the community become heightened. Neighbors may have casual discussions; there may be informal debates among leaders, or even something akin to town hall meetings. There may be kinds of analyses, field trips, or experimentation and prototypes. "Counting the cost" is a major focus in this phase since there may be some investment of resources required. Pros and cons are discussed to build confidence among the people. They are seeking to become convinced of its value.

The community goes through this phase to answer the question as to whether or not this change is really desired.

INTEGRATION PHASE:

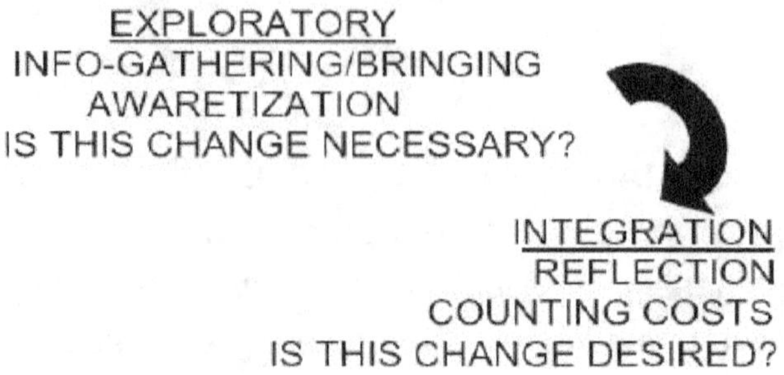

EXPLORATORY
INFO-GATHERING/BRINGING
AWARETIZATION
IS THIS CHANGE NECESSARY?

INTEGRATION
REFLECTION
COUNTING COSTS
IS THIS CHANGE DESIRED?

In the third phase, the ***DECISION*** phase, the people are attaining a level of interest to pursue possibilities for improvement. Leaders begin to emerge. High-level discussions get underway. Committees may be formed, available resources are considered, inventories taken, coordination and organization take form. Activities may include monitoring, encouraging, coaching, evaluating, multiplying, high- level organizing, encouraging participation, training, and planning. The people are in earnest to decide whether this change is possible.

DECISION PHASE:

EXPLORATORY
INFO-GATHERING/BRINGING
AWARETIZATION
IS THIS CHANGE NECESSARY??

INTEGRATION
REFLECTION
COUNTING COSTS
IS THIS CHANGE DESIRED?

DECISION
ORGANIZATION
IS THIS CHANGE POSSIBLE?

This continuing process may take significant time - perhaps weeks or many months -depending on the people's interest and progress.

Movement proceeds into the final phase called the ***PERFORMANCE*** phase. The community's hopes and aspirations are heading toward fulfillment as they move into action with full understanding of what they will do. The action required of them is very nearly contractual, as expectations of their level of participation need to be clear to all concerned.

Questions such as who will benefit (the entire community, especially the poor, not just a few elite), who will participate, who pays for what, who will maintain the project when the community development facilitators leave, are all questions that will have been addressed before actual work begins.

Having agreement as to what the people will do is critical. The project can move forward, with necessary modifications and adjustments being made along the way, to completion and a quick success.

PERFORMANCE PHASE:

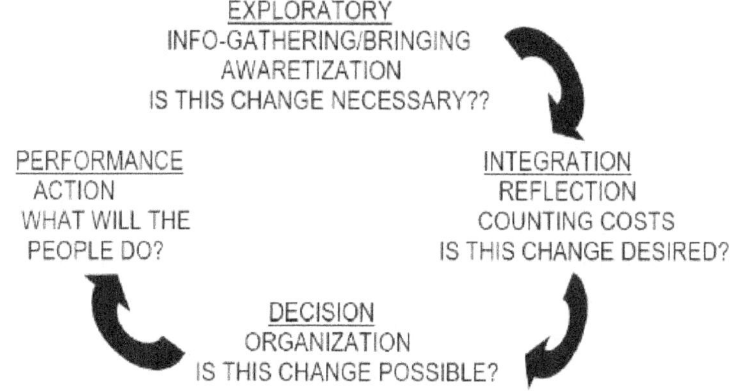

AND WHAT ABOUT THE COMMUNITY DEVELOPER?

As for the community development practitioner, we are prompted to ask, "*Where is your arrow"* in this revolving scheme of things?

The community development worker has been guiding all the action and discussion by *motivating* and *facilitating* the people.

As one success has been achieved, the next phase begins a new undertaking for another improvement. The same process is repeated as the next cycle begins anew.

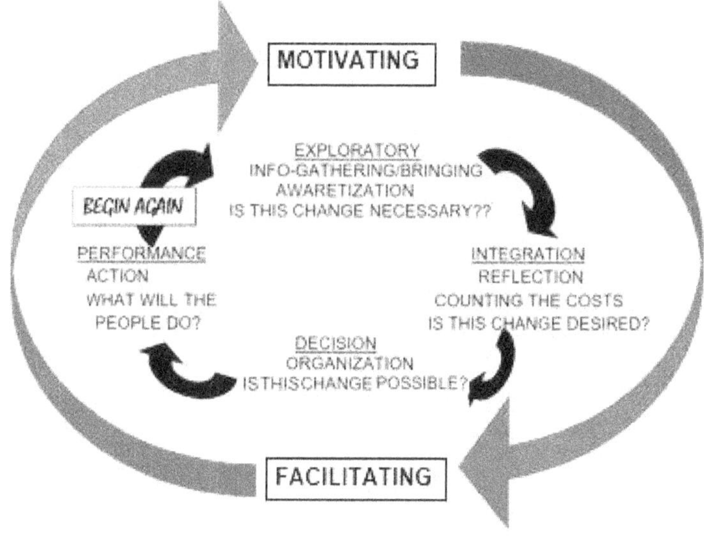

BUT WAIT! Before we plunge on to our next endeavor, it is essentially good practice to **"celebrate"** the recent victory. Recognizing the success of the poor community with ample attention to their accomplishment serves to encourage and stimulate them to perhaps even greater efforts in the future. One success is not development, but it begins the upward development spiral.

I learned this important principle of celebration from the Cambodian refugees we served in Thailand. Through our project, a band of refugees manufactured the huge water jars for the thousands of other refugees in the camps for the storage and conservation of water.

Following the completion of our project, our refugee workers themselves suggested we highlight the great achievement in the production of the water jars by organizing some kind of celebration. I loved the idea and requisitioned some funds for food, drinks and other amenities. I invited other leaders to celebrate with us to give the refugees added recognition. We handed out certificates of appreciation in a kind of graduation ceremony with full details printed, including their names, dates, and the name of the water jar project.

Thus, as the people's accomplishment is acknowledged through celebration, we are prepared to move on to the next improvement.

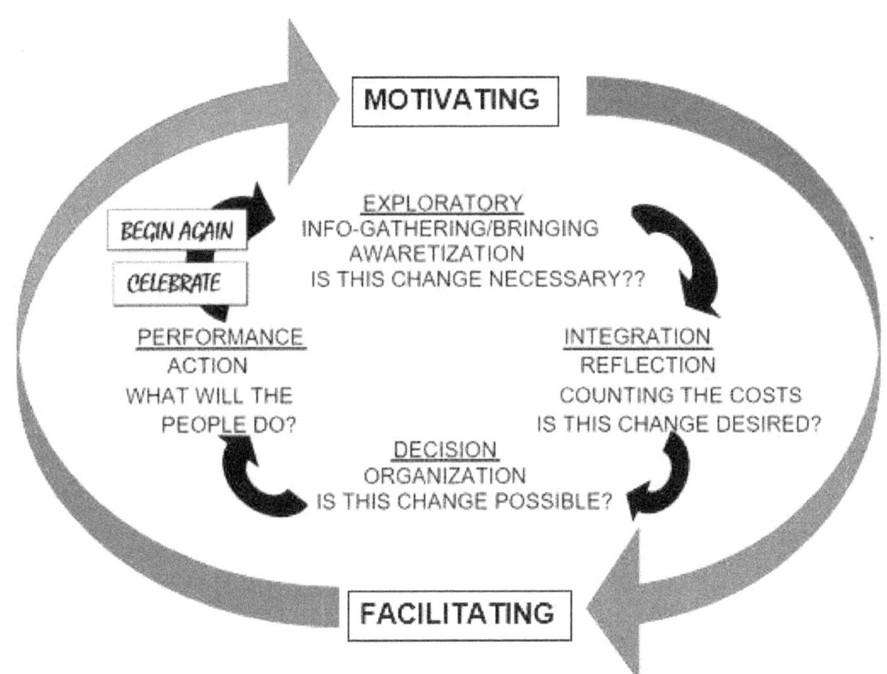

If you leave the people with no other accomplishment other than this process, you have moved them toward development. One change will not solve all the community's problems. Each change, however, opens the door to other changes to eventually transform the entire community.

There is the story of a development team that traveled via plane, train, and then boat for three days to get to their village destination in the Solomon Islands. By previous agreements with the village elders, they were to facilitate the building of a water tower for storage of water during the rainy season. Having followed all the obliging protocols over the team's outreach time, the water tower was built and finished three days before the team's departure homeward. During the village celebration on the tower's completion, the supporting platform gave way under the weight of the tower, and it came crashing down.

The shock brought grief and sadness to the team and some of them even wept. They felt their entire outreach and accomplishments were wasted as there was no time for repair or reconstruction of the tower with their departure time looming.

The village chief spoke and asked, "Why are you weeping? You have shown us what to do and how to build the tower. Don't weep. We will take care of it."

The following year, when the team returned to the village, there were two water towers.

BIBLIOGRAPHY:

Batchelor, Peter. *People in Rural Development.* Exeter, Devon, UK: The Paternoster Press, 1981.

Bunch, Roland. *Two Ears of Corn.* Oklahoma City, OK: World Neighbors, 1982.

Chamlee-Wright, Emily. *The Cultural Foundation of Economic Development.* New York: Routledge, 1997.

Cunningham, Loren. and Rogers, Janice. *Is That Really You, God?* Kona, HI: YWAM Publishing. 2nd ed. 2001.

Elliston, Edgar J., ed. *Christian Relief and Development.* Dallas, TX: Word Publishing, 1989.

Harrison, Lawrence E. and Huntington, Samuel P. eds. *Culture Matters.* New York: Basic Books, 2000.

Larsen, Dale and Sandy. *While Creation Waits.* Wheaton, IL: Harold Shaw Publishers, 1992.

Linthicum, Robert C. *Empowering the Poor.* Monrovia, CA: Marc Publishers, 1991.

Olson, Bruce E. *Bruchko.* Altamonte Springs, FL: Creation House, 1978.

Ward, Ted. *Living Overseas.* New York: The Free Press, 1984.

Wolters, Albert M. *Creation Regained.* Grand Rapids, MI: Wm. B. Eerdmans Publishing Co., 1985.

[A CRITIQUE]

Nunez C., Emilio A. *Liberation Theology.* trans. by Paul E. Sywulka. Chicago: Moody Press, 1985.

ABOUT THE AUTHOR

JOSEPH A. ROGOWSKI

Mr. Rogowski is a native of Buffalo, New York where he studied ancient classics in high school. He is a graduate pharmacist of the University of Buffalo, 1959. He met Ursula while she was visiting from Germany on an extended vacation, and they were married in 1963.

While enjoying a successful career as a pharmacist and minor partner in a regional chain of pharmacies in Western New York, Mr. Rogowski experienced a religious conversion in 1977. He resigned his positions in the company and left with Ursula and their two children for the mission field with Youth with a Mission in 1981. They served in Asia and the Pacific region for approximately ten years.

While on staff at the University of Nations in Kona, Hawaii, Mr. Rogowski developed a seminar on community development that eventually launched him into ministry with invitations for its presentation in fourteen different nations over two decades.

He earned a master's degree in public policy through studies at Regent University in Virginia Beach, Virginia in 1999 and taught a master's level course on Third World Politics at the International University in Vienna, Austria in 2001.

Joseph and Ursula served on Mercy Ships in Ghana in 2006 and in Liberia in 2008. While serving as a pharmacist aboard ship, during free time, Mr. Rogowski also presented seminars on community development to various church and interested groups in the local communities. He continues to promote the principles of helping the poor through community development and of a biblical worldview and culture.

He and Ursula have three grandchildren, three great-grandchildren and reside in suburban Richmond, Virginia.

They are directors of the small-project consulting, non-profit corporation, Arise Development Services.

Contact info: e-mail - heyrogo@verizon.net
www.mindingthetimes.com
www.arisedevelopmentservices.com
www.christiantrainingseminar.com
Facebook: Joseph Rogowski

This manual is an apologetic, autobiographical, technical, and philosophical blend to give the reader an informative, practical, instructive, and entertaining learning experience. It recounts some life experiences on the mission field that few have rarely encountered.

Here is a beginners look at the first principles of stimulating development among the poor to help themselves. Highlighted are the principles to effectively motivate and facilitate poor communities to become more self-reliant while avoiding the snares of dependency.

It is a must-read for those involved in service agency and ministry-oriented situations comprising groups of any type. It is a valuable tool for educators, industry professionals, business leaders, NGOs, generally service-minded organizations, and those considering mission outreach.

ISBN: 978-1-962142-80-9

www.ingramcontent.com/pod-product-compliance
Lightning Source LLC
Chambersburg PA
CBHW081700120626
46550CB00010B/2965

* 9 7 8 1 9 6 2 1 4 2 8 0 9 *